French
BUSINESS
PHRASE BOOK

D0972083

Easy to use features

Handy thematic colour coding

•

Quick reference pronunciation guide — opposite page

•

Country factfiles – inside back cover

•

Question and multiple response indicators throughout

How best to use this Phrase Book

This business phrase book has been designed to provide the handiest reference source to suit your business needs — whether you're on a trip to a French-speaking country, entertaining a French-speaking visitor, or corresponding by telephone, fax or letter with a French-speaking business partner.

- Consult the **Contents** pages (3-4) to locate the section you need. Separate, descriptive contents lists are included at the beginning of each chapter, to help you find your way around.

- Your fastest look-up is via the **English-French dictionary** (pp. 125-160), which contains over 2,500 essential business terms. For help in translating French documents, use the **French-English dictionary** (pp.161-191).

- For more technical terminology, consult **Industries and professions** (pp. 97-124). This section contains specific terms for use in 12 major business fields.

- Practical guidelines and the essential phrases for telephoning and introducing yourself and your company are provided in the section on **Making contact** (pp. 5-32).

- For more complex business situations, consult **Communication skills** (pp. 33-64). Sequenced phrases provide a progressive framework for developing meetings and negotiations successfully.

- For day-to-day business transactions, **Company departments** (pp. 65-96) provides the essential terms and model phrases for dealing effectively with your French-speaking counterpart.

Note: where applicable, feminine forms appear in parentheses, e.g. **assuré(e)**: feminine adjective *assurée*. With nouns, the appropriate feminine article should be substituted, e.g. **le directeur(-trice)**: feminine noun *la directrice*.

First edition 1996   Printed in Spain

CONTENTS

Acknowledgements

This material was developed in association with Nick Brieger and
Jeremy Comfort of York Associates, and JOHN GREEN TEFL TAPES;
business dictionaries were compiled by Peter Collin Publishing Ltd; our
thanks also to Able Translations Ltd – a division of Berlitz International
Inc. and Oxford Brookes Language Services for their help in the
preparation of this book.

Making Contact

BUSINESS COMMUNICATION

On the Telephone

A telephone directory of businesses and services can be obtained on *Minitel* – a network of telecommunications terminals installed in homes and businesses throughout France.

answering machine	**le répondeur téléphonique**
code	**le préfixe**
conference call	**l'audioconférence** *f*/**la teléconférence** *f*
dial (v)	**composer un numéro**
direct line	**la ligne directe**
engaged / busy	**en ligne/occupé(e)**
extension	**le poste**
get through	**obtenir la communication**
international call	**un appel international**
local call	**un appel régional**
look up a number	**chercher un numéro**
switchboard	**le standard**
telephone (n)/(v)	**le téléphone/téléphoner**
telephone directory	**l'annuaire** *m*

Identifying yourself

● Hello, ... Co./Inc. here.	● **Allô. Ici la société ...**
▶ Good morning/afternoon (sir/madam).	▶ **Bonjour monsieur/madame.**
▶ My name is ...	▶ **Je m'appelle/Mon nom est ...**
▶ This is ... here.	▶ **C'est ... à l'appareil.**

INTRODUCTIONS, see page 23

Asking to speak to someone

Could I speak to … please?	**Pourrais-je parler à …, s'il vous plaît?**
Could you put me through to … please?	**Pouvez-vous me passer …, s'il vous plaît?**
Can I have extension 351 please?	**Puis-je avoir le poste numéro 351, s'il vous plaît?**
Could I speak to someone who deals with …?	**Pourrais-je parler à quelqu'un qui s'occupe de …?**
▶Who's calling?	▶**Qui est à l'appareil?/De la part de qui?**
▶Could you tell me what it's about?	▶**Pourriez-vous me dire de quoi il s'agit?**
▶Can I help you?	▶**Puis-je vous aider?**
▶Who would you like to speak to?	▶**À qui désirez-vous parler?**
▶Speaking.	▶**C'est moi-même.**

Giving the reason for the call

It's in connection with …	**Cela concerne …**
It's about …	**C'est au sujet de …**
I'm calling about …	**J'appelle au sujet de …**
I'm phoning to tell you …	**Je téléphone pour vous dire que …**

Making excuses

I'm afraid _____ is …	**Je suis désolé(e), _____ est …**
not available at the moment.	**occupé pour l'instant.**
in a meeting.	**en réunion.**
with a customer at the moment.	**en ce moment avec un client.**
I'm sorry but _____ …	**Je suis désolé(e), mais _____ …**
is on holiday/vacation.	**est en congé/en vacances.**
is not in the office.	**n'est pas au bureau.**
is on the other line at present.	**est actuellement en communication.**
is no longer with the company.	**ne fait plus partie de notre société.**
I'm afraid his line's engaged/busy.	**Je suis désolé(e), son poste est occupé.**
Do you want to hold?	**Voulez-vous patienter?**
Can I pass you to his …	**Puis-je vous passer son/sa …**
assistant/colleague/replacement	**assistant(e)/collègue/remplaçant(e)**

INTRODUCING YOUR COMPANY, see page 28 & 45

Taking a message

Would you like to leave a message?	Désirez-vous transmettre un message?
May I take a message?	Puis-je prendre un message?
Can I take your name and number?	Pourriez-vous me laisser vos coordonnées?
Can I get him to call you back?	Désirez-vous qu'il vous rappelle?

Leaving a message

Could you give him a message?	Pourriez-vous lui transmettre un message?
Could you ask her to call me back?	Pourriez-vous lui demander de me rappeler?
Could you tell her I'll call back later?	Pourriez-vous lui dire que je la rappellerai plus tard?

Showing you understand

I see.	Je vois.
I understand.	Je comprends.
Right/Fine/Okay.	D'accord/Bien/O.k.

Communication problems

Could you repeat that?	Pourriez-vous répéter?
I'm sorry, I didn't catch your name.	Je suis désolé(e), je n'ai pas compris votre nom.
Could you speak a little slower/louder?	Pourriez-vous parler un peu plus lentement/fort?
It's a very bad line. I'll call you back.	La ligne est très mauvaise. Je vous rappellerai.
Could you spell that please?	Pourriez-vous épeler ce mot, s'il vous plaît?
Let me just repeat that …	Si j'ai bien compris …

Ending the call

Thanks very much for your help.	Merci beaucoup pour votre aide.
I look forward …	J'espère …
to seeing you soon.	vous voir prochainement.
hearing from you.	avoir de vos nouvelles.
See you soon.	À bientôt.
Goodbye/Bye.	Au-revoir.
Thanks for calling.	Merci d'avoir appelé.

TELEPHONE NUMBERS, see page 18

Business Communication

MAKING CONTACT

Correspondence

Business correspondence is very formal in French and the use of a number of set expressions is required for commencing and closing a letter. A typical letter would be addressed:

GILLOT S.A.

Fabricants de meubles

```
Monsieur BRETON
Société N.B.F.
89, avenue de Lilas
44000 NANTES
```

Vos références: MT/354
Nos références: LE/MFB
Objet: Demande de rensignements

```
Genéve, le 7 mars 199-
```

A more straightforward style can be used in faxes and telexes.

Dubois et fils   *Télécopie*

Société/Destinataire: Worldwines
A l'attention de: Peter Brown
N° de Fax: + 44 01234 683445
De/Expediteur: Pierre Dubois
Nombre de pages: 1
Date: 23 Mars 199-

The greeting

to a firm:	**Messieurs**
to an unknown individual:	**Monsieur, Madame**
to a known individual:	**Monsieur/Madame/ Mademoiselle**
to a prominent individual	**Monsieur le Président/Madame la Directrice** *etc*
to an acquaintance:	**Chère Madame/Cher Monsieur Dubois** *etc*

Business Communication

The start

Thank you for your letter of _____ (*date*), ...	**En vous remerciant pour votre courrier du _____, ...**
I have received your letter of _____ (*date*), ...	**J'ai bien reçu votre courrier du _____, ...**
asking if/about ...	**demandant si/au sujet de ...**
concerning ...	**concernant ...**
in which you asked ...	**dans lequel vous demandiez ...**

Explaining the purpose

We are writing to enquire/ inquire about/whether ...	**Nous vous écrivons pour nous renseigner sur/vous demander si ...**
I am writing in connection with ...	**Je vous écris au sujet de ...**
In response to ...	**En réponse à ...**
With reference to ...	**Faisant référence à ...**
Further to ...	**Concernant ...**
With regard to ...	**Au sujet de ...**

Requesting

We would be very grateful if you could ...	**Nous vous serions reconnaissants si vous pouviez ...**
I would be much obliged if you could ...	**Je vous serais reconnaissant(e) si vous pouviez ...**
We would appreciate it if you could ...	**Nous serions heureux si vous pouviez ...**
Please could you ... (*informal*)	**Pourriez-vous, s'il vous plaît, ...**

Giving information or replying to a request for information

Positive

Please find enclosed ...	**Veuillez trouver ci-joint ...**
We are happy to enclose ...	**Nous avons le plaisir de vous envoyer ci-joint ...**
We wish to inform you that ...	**Nous souhaitons vous informer que ...**
We are pleased to inform you that ...	**Nous avons le plaisir de vous informer que ...**

Negative

We regret to inform you that ...	**Nous sommes au regret de vous informer que ...**

We are sorry to tell you that ...	Nous sommes désolés de vous annoncer que ...

Thanking

I am much obliged to you for sending me ...	Je vous remercie de m'avoir fait parvenir ...
I am grateful to you for ...	Je vous remercie de ...
We are much obliged to you for ...	Nous vous remercions de ...
Thank you for ... *(informal)*	Merci de ...

Apologizing

We were extremely sorry to hear about the problem.	Nous avons été désolés d'apprendre l'existence de ce problème.
We regret that this problem has happened.	Nous regrettons que ce problème soit apparu.
We apologise for ...	Veuillez nous excuser de ...

Linking ideas

The following linking words can make your letter easier to read.

Cause
therefore/so/consequently donc/ainsi/par conséquent

Comparison
similarly/in the same way de même/de la même manière

Contrast
however/nevertheless cependant/néanmoins

Addition
in addition/also/too de plus/également/aussi

Equivalence
in other words/that means en d'autres termes/c'est-à-dire

Inclusion
for example/e.g. par exemple/ex.
such as/as follows comme/comme suit

Highlight	
in particular/especially/mainly	**en particulier/surtout/ principalement**
Generalization	
usually/normally/as a rule	**d'habitude/normalement/en règle générale**
Stating the obvious	
obviously/naturally/of course	**manifestement/naturellement/ bien entendu**
Summary	
in summary/to sum up	**en résumé/pour résumer**
overall/in brief	**dans l'ensemble en bref/ en résumé**
Conclusion	
in conclusion/finally/lastly	**en conclusion/finalement/pour finir**

The closing

Please don't hesitate to contact us if you need any further information.	**N'hésitez pas à nous contacter pour de plus amples informations.**
We look forward to hearing from you/meeting you.	**Dans l'attente d'une réponse de votre part/de vous recontrer.**
We look forward to receiving the proposal/your order/your reply.	**Dans l'attente de votre offre/ commande/réponse.**

The farewell

French equivalents of "Yours sincerely", "With best regards" etc. are expansive, as these examples show:

Veuillez agréer, Madame, l'expression de mes salutations distinguées

Nous vous prions de croire, Messieurs, à l'assurance de nos sentiments distinguées

Je vous prie de croire, Monsieur, en l'assurance de mes sentiments les meilleurs *(shows more warmth)*

Meilleurs salutations/Sincèrement vôtre *(less formal, for faxes)*

The enclosures

Encl.	**ci-joint, p.j. (piéce(s) jointe(s))**

ARRANGING APPOINTMENTS

appointment	**le rendez-vous**
calendar	**le calendrier**
date	**la date**
diary	**l'agenda** *m*
engagement	**le rendez-vous**
meeting	**la réunion**
schedule	**le programme**
timetable	**l'emploi** *m* **du temps**

Opening

You may remember, we met at ...

Vous vous souvenez peut-être que nous nous sommes rencontrés lors de ...

... suggested I contact you.
I feel we should get together.

... m'a proposé de vous contacter.
Je pense que nous devrions nous entendre.

Mr/Mrs .... said he/she would like to talk about ...
I'd like to tell you about ...
I'd like to arrange a meeting.
Let's fix a date.
Could we meet?

M./Mme ... m'a dit qu'il/elle souhaite discuter au sujet de ...
Je voudrais vous informer sur ...
Je voudrais prendre rendez-vous.
Convenons d'une date.
Pourrions-nous nous rencontrer?

● Could you tell me what it's about?
● Why do want to see Monsieur Dupont?
▶ I'd like to discuss ...
▶ We need to talk about ...

● **Pourriez-vous me dire de quoi il s'agit?**
● **Pourquoi souhaitez-vous rencontrer Monsieur Dupont?**
▶ **Je voudrais discuter de ...**
▶ **Nous devons parler de ...**

Arranging a time

Could you manage next week?

La semaine prochaine vous convient-elle?

What about Friday afternoon?

Vendredi après-midi vous convient-il?

Would Monday suit you?
Shall we say 2 o'clock?
▶ I'm afraid I can't manage Friday.
▶ Next week is out.

Lundi vous conviendrait-il?
Disons 14 heures?
▶ **Je suis désolé, mais vendredi ne me convient pas.**
▶ **La semaine prochaine, c'est exclu.**

DATES, see page 15/TIME, see page 16

Arranging Appointments

▶ Can you make the following week?	▶ Pouvez-vous la semaine d'après?
▶ Tuesday would suit me better.	▶ Mardi me conviendrait mieux.
▶ 4 o'clock would be fine.	▶ 16 heures c'est parfait.

Duration

It'll have to be short. I've got another meeting at 5.	Notre entretien devra être court. J'ai un autre rendez-vous à 17 heures.
It won't take more than an hour.	Cela ne prendra pas plus d'une heure.

Place

Where do you suggest?	Où proposez-vous de nous rencontrer?
I'll come to your office.	Je viendrai à votre bureau.
Shall we meet in my office?	Voulez-vous que nous nous rencontrions dans mon bureau?

Directions

Can you give me some directions?	Pouvez-vous me donner quelques indications?
Will you be coming by car?	Viendrez-vous en voiture?
I would take a taxi from the airport.	Je prendrais un taxi à l'aéroport.
I'll fax you a map.	Je vous enverrai un plan par fax.
Just ask for me at the reception desk.	Demandez-moi à l'accueil.
My office is on the fifth floor (*US* sixth floor).	Mon bureau est au cinquième étage.

Ending

Let me just confirm that. Friday 24th, 3:30 at your office.	Alors je confirme: vendredi le 24, à 15 heures 30 à votre bureau.
I look forward to seeing you then.	Je suis impatient(e) de vous rencontrer.
See you next Friday.	À vendredi prochain.

En route

Where can I get a taxi?	Où puis-je prendre un taxi?
Could you take me to …?	Pouvez-vous m'amener à …?

TRAVELLING AROUND, see page 19

- Could you tell me how to get to ...?
- Where can I park?
  - Straight ahead.
  - Turn left/right.
  - You'll see it on your right.

- Pouvez-vous m'indiquer comment aller à ...?
- Où puis-je me garer?
  - Tout droit.
  - Tournez à gauche/droite.
  - Vous le verrez sur votre droite.

Arriving

My name's ...
I've got an appointment with ...
  - Please take a seat.
  - Mr ... will see you now.

  - She'll be with you shortly.

Je m'appelle ...
J'ai un rendez-vous avec ...
  - Prenez place s'il vous plaît.
  - M. ... peut vous recevoir maintenant.
  - Elle sera avec vous dans un instant.

Cancelling an appointment

Unfortunately, I'll have to cancel our meeting on ...
I'll be unable to make the meeting.
- Can we fix a new time? How about ...?

  - I'll check.
  - I'm afraid that's not possible.

Malheureusement, je dois annuler notre rendez-vous de ...
Je serais dans l'impossibilité de tenir notre rendez-vous.
- Pouvons-nous convenir d'une nouvelle heure? ... vous conviendrait-il?

  - Je vais vérifier.
  - J'ai peur que cela ne soit pas possible.

Months

January	janvier
February	février
March	mars
April	avril
May	mai
June	juin
July	juillet
August	août
September	septembre
October	octobre
November	novembre
December	décembre

Date

● What is the date today?	● Quel jour sommes nous?
▶ It's March 1st.	▶ Nous sommes le premier mars.
April 5th	le cinq april
in May	en mai
on September 7	le sept septembre
from June to August	de juin à août
at the beginning of October	le début (d')octobre
in the middle of July	la mi-juillet
at the end of November	la fin (de) novembre

Years

1996	mille neuf cent quatre-vingt seize
1998	mille neuf cent quatre-vingt dix-huit
in 2001	en meux mille un

Days

Monday	lundi
Tuesday	mardi
Wednesday	mercredi
Thursday	jeudi
Friday	vendredi
Saturday	samedi
Sunday	dimanche

today	aujourd'hui
tomorrow	demain
yesterday	hier
the day before yesterday	avant-hier
the day after tomorrow	après-demain
this Wednesday	ce mercredi
next Friday	vendredi prochain
a week on from Tuesday	mardi en huit
by Thursday	d'ici jeudi
on Saturday	samedi
every Monday/on Mondays	chaque lundi/les lundis
in 5 days' time	dans cinq jours
last/next month	le mois dernier/prochain
for 5 days	pour cinq jours

NUMBERS, see page 17

Times of day

early morning	tôt le matin
morning	le matin
midday	le midi
lunchtime	l'heure *f* du déjeuner
before lunch	avant le déjeuner
after lunch	après le déjeuner
afternoon	l'après-midi *m*
late afternoon	la fin d'après-midi
evening	le soir

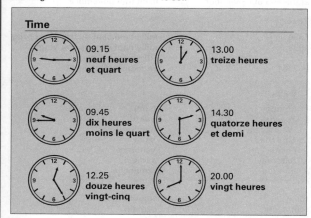

Time

09.15
**neuf heures
et quart**

13.00
treize heures

09.45
**dix heures
moins le quart**

14.30
**quatorze heures
et demi**

12.25
**douze heures
vingt-cinq**

20.00
vingt heures

● What time does it start/end?

▶ at 9.15 am
● How long will it last?

▶ 10 minutes
▶ ¾ of an hour
▶ until 7.30 pm
▶ from ... up to ...
  about ...
  ... exactly
  ... at the latest

● **À quelle heure cela commence-
t-il/se termine-t-il?**
▶ **à neuf heures quinze du matin**
● **Combien de temps cela
va-t-il durer?**
▶ **dix minutes**
▶ **trois quarts d'heure**
▶ **jusqu'à 19h30**
▶ **de ... à ...**
  vers ...
  ... pile
  ... au plus tard

Numbers

0	zéro	30	trente
1	un/une	40	quarante
2	deux	50	cinquante
3	trois	60	soixante
4	quatre	70	soixante-dix
5	cinq	80	quatre-vingts
6	six	90	quatre-vingt-dix
7	sept	100	cent
8	huit	110	cent dix
9	neuf	200	deux cents
10	dix	300	trois cents
11	onze	400	quatre cents
12	douze	500	cinq cents
13	treize	1000	mille
14	quattorze	1100	mille cent
15	quinze	1200	mille deux cents
16	seize	2000	deux mille
17	dix-sept	5000	cinq mille
18	dix-huit	10,000	dix mille
19	dix-neuf	50,000	cinquante mille
20	vingt	100,000	cent mille
21	vingt et un	1,000,000	un million
22	vingt-deux	1,000,000,000	un milliard

Note: In Belgium and Switzerland, **septante** (70), **huitante** (80) and **nonante** (90) are used.

Ordinal numbers

first (1st)	premier (1er)
second (2nd)	deuxième (2e)
third (3rd)	troisième (3e)
fourth	quatrième
fifth	cinquième
sixth	sixième
seventh	septième
eighth	huitième
ninth	neuvième
tenth	dixième
hundredth	centième
millionth	millionième

Fractions etc.

a half	**une moitié**
half (adj)	**demi(e)**
a quarter	**un quart**
one third	**un tiers**
four fifths	**quatre cinquièmes**
three point four (3.4)	**trois virgule quatre (3,4)**
once/twice/three times	**une fois/deux fois/trois fois**

Telephone numbers

Telephone numbers are usually read in pairs.

00 33 - 1 - 45-25-78-14	**zero zero, trente-trois, un, quarante-cinq, vingt-cinq, soixante-dix-huit, quattorze**

Money

10,523.50 French francs	**dix mille cinq cent vingt-trois francs cinquante (FFr 10.523,50)**
$10 per unit	**dix dollars par unité**
profits have doubled/trebled/ halved	**les bénéfices ont doublé/triplé/ diminué de moitié**

Reference numbers

254/DG	**deux cent cinquante-quatre barre DG**
3580-00	**trois mille cinq cent quatre-vingts tiret zéro zéro**

Measurements

1.2 metres/meters	**un virgule deux mètres (1,2m)**
500 litres/liters	**cinq cent litres**
about 20 stores	**environ vingt magasins**
in the region of $7/8$ths	**aux alentours du sept/huitièmes**
between 50 and 60 percent	**entre cinquante et soixante pour cent**
30-40,000	**trente à quarante mille**
sales have dropped/risen by 30,000 units	**les ventes ont chuté/augmenté de trente mille unités**

TRAVELLING AROUND

Travel by plane

Is there a connecting flight to …?	Y-a-t-il une correspondance pour …?
When does it leave/take off?	À quelle heure est le départ/le décollage?
When does it arrive/land?	À quelle heure est l'arrivée/ l'atterrissage?
What time do I have to check in?	À quelle heure est l'enregistrement?
Is it a direct flight?	Est-ce un vol direct?

Booking and changing flights

ticket	le billet
single/one-way	aller simple
economy class	classe économique
business class	classe affaires
I'd like to book a return/round-trip flight to …	Je voudrais réserver un vol aller-retour pour …
I'd like to cancel/change my reservation on flight number …	Je voudrais annuler/changer ma réservation sur le vol numéro …

Travel by train

platform	le quai
ticket office	le guichet
ticket reservations	les réservations f des billets
timetable	l'horaire m

Enquiring about rail travel

When is the next train to …?	Quand part le prochain train pour …?
What's the fare to …?	Quel est le prix du voyage à …?
Do I have to change?	Dois-je changer de train?
When does it arrive at …?	À quelle heure le train arrive-t-il à …?
Which platform does the train leave from/arrive at?	Sur quel quai part/arrive le train?

Buying a ticket

I'd like a single/one-way ticket to ...	Je voudrais un aller simple pour ...
return/round trip	aller-retour *m*
first-class	première classe
I'd like to reserve a seat.	Je voudrais réserver ma place.

On the train

buffet/restaurant car	le buffet/le wagon-restaurant
couchette/sleeping car	la couchette/le wagon-lits
first-class compartment	le compartiment première classe
Is this the right train to ...?	Est-ce le train pour ...?
Is this seat taken?	Cette place est-elle prise?
I think that's my seat.	Je pense que c'est ma place.

Travel by taxi

Could you get me a taxi?	Pouvez-vous m'appeler un taxi?
Where is the taxi rank/stand?	Où est la station de taxis?
Take me to ...	Conduisez-moi ...
the Trade Fair	à la foire exposition
this address	à cette adresse
Please stop here.	Arrêtez-vous ici, s'il vous plaît.
Could you wait for me?	Pourriez-vous m'attendre?
I'll be back in 10 minutes.	Je serai de retour dans dix minutes.
How much do I owe you?	Combien est-ce-que je vous dois?
Keep the change.	Gardez la monnaie.

Travel by car

Car hire/rental

I'd like to hire/rent a car.	Je voudrais louer une voiture.
medium-sized	une voiture moyenne
automatic	une automatique
with air-conditioning	avec climatisation
Is mileage included?	Le kilométrage est-il inclus?
I'd like to leave the car in ...	J'aimerais laisser la voiture à ...
How much is the deposit?	La caution se monte à combien?
I'd like full insurance.	J'aimerais une assurance tous risques.

At the petrol/gas station

Could you fill it up, please?	**Pourriez-vous faire le plein, s'il vous plaît?**
petrol/gasoline	**l'essence** *f*
regular/premium/unleaded	**normal/super/sans plomb**

Garage–Breaking down

My car's broken down.	**Ma voiture est en panne.**
May I use your phone?	**Puis-je utiliser votre téléphone?**
My car won't start.	**Ma voiture ne démarre plus.**
The battery is dead.	**La batterie est à plat.**
I've run out of petrol.	**Je suis en panne sèche.**
I've got a flat tyre/tire.	**J'ai crevé un pneu.**
There's something wrong with the brakes.	**J'ai un problème de frein.**
Please check the ...	**Vérifiez s'il vous plaît ...**
battery	**la batterie**
spare tyre/tire	**la roue de secours**
tyre/tire pressure	**la pression des pneus**

Accidents

Where's the nearest ...?	**Où est ... le plus proche?**
telephone/garage	**le téléphone/le garagiste**
Could you call an ambulance?	**Pouvez-vous appeler une ambulance?**
Here's my driving licence/ driver's license.	**Voici mon permis de conduire.**
What's your name and address?	**Quels sont vos nom et adresse?**
What's your insurance company.	**Quelle est votre compagnie d'assurance?**

Directions

Go straight ahead.	**Allez tout droit.**
It's on the left/right.	**C'est sur votre gauche/droite.**
opposite/behind ...	**en face de/derrière ...**
next to/after ...	**à côté de/après ...**
Turn left at the ...	**Tournez à gauche ...**
next corner	**au prochain tournant**
traffic lights	**au feu rouge/aux feux**
Take the N3.	**Prenez la N3.**
You have to go back to ...	**Vous devez retourner à ...**

Accommodation

Booking a room

I'd like a single room for 2 nights.	**Je voudrais une chambre simple pour deux nuits.**
From ... to ...	**De ... à ...**
single room	**chambre simple**
double room	**chambre double**
twin-bedded room	**chambre à deux lits**
family room	**chambre familiale**
with bath/shower	**avec baignoire** f **/douche** f
It must be quiet.	**Elle doit être calme.**
I'll be arriving late.	**J'arriverai tard.**
How much does it cost?	**Quel est le prix?**
Do you accept credit cards?	**Acceptez-vous les cartes de crédit?**

Registering at a hotel

● My name's ...	● **Je m'appelle ...**
● I've a reservation for 2 nights.	● **J'ai réservé pour deux nuits.**
▶ Could you fill in this form?	▶ **Pouvez-vous remplir ce formulaire?**
▶ How will you be paying?	▶ **Comment désirez-vous régler votre note?**
▶ May I see your credit card?	▶ **Puis-je voir votre carte de crédit?**

Complaining

Could I have a quieter room?	**Pourrais-je avoir une chambre plus calme?**
My room's too small/noisy.	**Ma chambre est trop petite/ bruyante.**

Checking out

May I have the bill please?	**Pouvez-vous me faire ma note, s'il vous plaît?**
You've made a mistake in this bill.	**Vous avez fait une erreur dans ma note.**
Can you order a taxi please?	**Pouvez-vous m'appeler un taxi, s'il vous plaît?**

DATES, see page 15

INTRODUCTIONS

In business, people generally call each other **Monsieur/Madame** or
Mademoiselle + surname. Christian names are used only after
knowing each other well. Shake hands when you meet and leave;
business cards are exchanged at the beginning of the meeting.

Greetings

Hello.	**Bonjour.**
Good morning/afternoon.	**Bonjour.**
Good evening.	**Bonsoir.**
How do you do?	**Enchanté(e).**
Pleased to meet you.	**Je suis enchanté(e) de faire votre connaissance.**

Introducing yourself

My name's ...	**Je m'appelle ...**
I'm ...	**Je suis ...**
Please call me ...	**Appelez-moi ... s'il vous plaît.**
Everybody calls me ...	**Tout le monde m'appelle ...**

Responding

How do you do? I'm ...	**Enchanté(e). Je suis ...**
Pleased to meet you too. My name is ...	**Enchanté(e). Je m'appelle ...**
Nice to meet you too.	**Je suis enchanté(e) de faire votre connaissance.**

Introducing others

Peter, this is ...	**Peter, voici ...**
May I introduce you to ...	**Puis-je vous présenter ...**
Have you two met? This is ...	**Vous êtes-vous déjà rencontrés? Voici ...**

Everyday greetings

● How are you?	● **Comment allez-vous?**
▶ Fine, and you?	▶ **Bien, et vous?**
▶ Not so bad.	▶ **Pas si mal.**
▶ Could be worse.	▶ **Cela pourrait être pire.**

Presenting your job

- What do you do?
- What line are you in?

- I'm ...
  a secretary
  an accountant

- I work in ...
  an insurance company
  a school

- I work for ...
  IBM/the local newspaper
  a pharmaceutical company

- I'm on the ... side.
  technical/commercial
  administrative

- I'm in ...
  marketing
  sales/finance

- I'm ...
  self-employed/unemployed
  out of work/retired

- Que faites-vous?
- Dans quel domaine travaillez-vous?

- Je suis ...
  secrétaire *m/f*
  comptable *m*

- Je travaille dans ...
  une compagnie d'assurances
  une école

- Je travaille pour ...
  IBM/le journal régional
  une entreprise pharmaceutique

- Je suis dans le domaine ...
  technique/commercial
  administratif

- Je suis dans ...
  le marketing
  les ventes/les finances

- Je suis ...
  à mon compte/au chômage
  sans travail/à la retraite

Origins

- Where are you from?
- Where do you live?

- D'où êtes-vous?
- Où habitez-vous?

I come from ...	I'm ...	Je viens ...	Je suis ...
Austria	Austrian	d'Autriche	autrichien(ne)
Belgium	Belgian	de Belgique	belge
Britain	British	de Grande Bretagne	britannique
Canada	Canadian	du Canada	canadien(ne)
England	English	d'Angleterre	anglais(e)
France	French	de France	français(e)
Germany	German	d'Allemagne	allemand(e)
Ireland	Irish	d'Irlande	irlandais(e)
Scotland	Scottish	d'Ecosse	écossais(e)
Switzerland	Swiss	de Suisse	suisse
United States	American	des Etats-Unis	américain(e)
Wales	Welsh	du Pays de Galles	gallois(e)

COMPANY POSITIONS, see page 28

Socializing

After-work socializing is invariably conducted in a restaurant; an invitation to the home is rare. Punctuality is a rule of politeness; more than 15 minutes late is considered rude.

Arriving

● How was your trip?

▶ Not bad.
▶ No problems.
▶ Rather long.

● When did you arrive?
● When did you get in?
● Did you ...
  take the train/fly?
  come by car/drive?
▶ I came by car/I drove.
▶ I took the last flight.

● **Comment s'est passé votre voyage?**
▶ **Pas mal.**
▶ **Sans problèmes.**
▶ **Plutôt long.**

● **Quand êtes-vous arrivé(e)?**
● **Quand êtes-vous arrivé(e)?**
● **Avez-vous pris ...**
  le train/l'avion?
  la voiture?
▶ **Je suis venu(e) en voiture.**
▶ **J'ai pris le dernier vol.**

Leaving

● I'm leaving tomorrow.
▶ What time does your plane leave?
▶ When do you have to check in?

● **Je pars demain.**
▶ **À quelle heure part votre avion?**
▶ **À quelle heure devez-vous enregistrer vos bagages?**

Could you book a taxi for me?
I need a taxi to take me to the airport.
How long do you think it will take?

Pourriez-vous me réserver un taxi?
J'ai besoin d'un taxi qui m'amène à l'aéroport.
Combien de temps pensez-vous que cela va-t-il prendre?

Accommodation

● How's your hotel?

▶ Yes, it's fine.
▶ It's OK.
▶ It's a bit noisy.

● **Comment trouvez-vous votre hôtel?**
▶ **Oui, il est bien.**
▶ **Ça va.**
▶ **Il est un peu bruyant.**

Weather

What a lovely day!
What awful weather!

Quelle belle journée!
Quel temps horrible!

TRAVELLING AROUND, see page 19/ACCOMMODATION, see page 22

● What was the weather like when you left?
▶ Much the same as here.
▶ Very sunny.
▶ Dreadful.
▶ Lovely and warm.
▶ Cold for the time of year.

● Quel temps faisait-il quand vous êtes parti?
▶ Plus ou moins le même qu'ici.
▶ Très ensoleillé.
▶ Epouvantable.
▶ Beau et chaud.
▶ Froid pour la saison.

Family

● Are you married?
▶ Yes, my wife is …
▶ My husband is …
▶ No, I'm single.
▶ I'm divorced.

● Êtes-vous marié(e)?
▶ Oui, ma femme est …
▶ Mon mari est …
▶ Non, je suis célibataire.
▶ Je suis divorcé(e).

● Have you got any children?
▶ Yes, two boys and a girl.
▶ one daughter/three sons

● Avez-vous des enfants?
▶ Oui, deux garçons et une fille.
▶ une fille/trois fils

● How old are they?
▶ They're ten and twelve.
▶ The oldest is …
▶ The youngest is …
▶ Oh, they've left home.

● Quel âge ont-ils?
▶ Ils ont dix et douze ans.
▶ L'aîné(e) a …
▶ Le/La plus jeune a …
▶ Oh, ils ont quitté la maison.

Interests

● What do you do at/on the weekends?
● Are you interested in sports?
● Do you play any sports?
▶ I play football/golf/tennis.
▶ I don't play but I watch …

▶ I go fishing/swimming.

● Que faites-vous les week-ends?

● Le sport vous intéresse-t-il?
● Faites-vous du sport?
▶ Je joue au football/golf/tennis.
▶ Je n'en fais pas, mais je regarde …

▶ Je vais pêcher/nager.

Invitations

● Would you like to come to/for dinner?
▶ I'd love to./I'd like that.
▶ I'd love to but …
▶ I'm afraid I can't.

▶ I've got another engagement.

● Aimeriez-vous venir dîner à la maison?
▶ Avec plaisir./Oui, volontiers.
▶ J'aimerais bien, mais …
▶ Je suis désolé(e), je ne peux pas.
▶ Je suis pris(e).

● Could you manage next Tuesday?	● Pourriez-vous mardi prochain?
▶ Tuesday would be fine.	▶ Mardi, c'est parfait.
● How about a drink after work?	● Voulez-vous boire un verre après le travail?
▶ Good idea.	▶ Bonne idée.
● Let me buy you a drink.	● Laissez-moi vous offrir un verre.
▶ That's very kind of you.	▶ C'est très gentil de votre part.

Dining out

Arriving & ordering

We've booked a table for four.	Nous avons réservé une table pour quatre.
Are you having a starter/ a dessert?	Prenez-vous une entrée/un dessert?
I'd recommend the fish.	Je vous recommande le poisson.
What are you going to have?	Que prendrez-vous?
I think I'll have the beef.	Je crois que je vais prendre le bœuf.
Could you tell me what … is?	Pourriez-vous me dire ce qu'est …?

Commenting

The fish is delicious.	Le poisson est délicieux.
Are you enjoying the beef?	Aimez-vous le bœuf?
Thank you for a lovely meal.	Merci pour ce bon repas.

Paying

Could I have the bill?	Puis-je avoir l'addition?
Do you accept … card?	Acceptez-vous la carte …?
Is the service included?	Le service est-il inclus?

Saying goodbye

I'm afraid we must go now.	Je crains que nous devions partir maintenant.
I look forward to seeing you soon/again next year.	Je me réjouis de vous revoir bientôt/l'année prochaine.
Goodbye/See you soon.	Au revoir/À bientôt.

Introducing the company

French companies tend to be heirarchical; rank is considered very important.

Sectors

Heavy Industry	l'industrie *f* lourde
(Light) Manufacturing	l'industrie *f* légère
Services	les services *m*

Types of company

company	la société
firm	l'entreprise *f*
sole trader	le négociant exclusif
partnership	une association
limited company	une société à responsabilité limitée (S.A.R.L.)
public limited company/corporation	une société anonyme (S.A.)
general partnership	une société en nom collectif (S.N.C.)
state company	une entreprise d'État
private company	une société privée

Parts of company

Head Office/Headquarters	le siège social
Parent company	la maison mère
Holding company	un holding
Subsidiary	la filiale
Business Unit	l'unité *f* d'activité
Branch	la succursale
Sales Office	le service des ventes
Division	la division
Department	le service
Section	l'équipe *f*

Position in a company

Chairman	le président directeur général (le P.D.G.)
Managing Director/CEO/President	le directeur administratif, le directeur général
Vice President	le vice-président

PERSONNEL DEPARTMENT, see page 86

Director	**le directeur**
Manager	**le gérant**
Departmental head	**le chef de service**
Supervisor	**le responsable**
Assistant	**l'assistant(e)**
Shop floor worker	**l'ouvrier (-ère)**
Office staff	**l'employé(e) de bureau**

People in a company

headcount	**l'effectif** m
staff	**les employés** m
personnel	**le personnel**
senior management	**les cadres** m **supérieurs**
middle/lower	**moyens/subalternes**
workers	**les ouvriers** m, **la main d'œuvre**

People around the company

suppliers	**les fournisseurs** m
customers	**les clients** m
clients	**la clientèle**
agents	**les agents** m
distributors	**les distributeurs** m
dealers	**les négociants** m

Location

We're based in …	**Nous nous situons à …**
Our head office is located in …	**Notre siège se situe à …**
We have branches throughout the world.	**Nous avons des filiales dans le monde entier.**

Activity

We're in the telecommunications field.	**Nous sommes dans le domaine de la télécommunication.**
We're a leading company in …	**Nous sommes leaders dans le domaine de …**
There are three major business units.	**Il y a trois unités principales.**

Size

There are four partners in the firm.	**Il y a quatre associés dans l'entreprise.**

We employ 20,000 people.	**Nous employons 20 000 personnes.**
We have 20,000 employees.	**Nous avons 20 000 employés.**
We have an annual sales/ turnover of \$250 million.	**Nous réalisons un chiffre d'affaires annuel de 250 millions de dollars.**
Annual profits are in the region of \$25 million.	**Les bénéfices annuels sont de l'ordre de 25 millions de dollars.**

Career development

I started as a foreman on the shop floor.	**J'ai commencé en tant que contremaître dans l'usine.**
I got promoted to plant manager.	**J'ai été promu(e) en tant que directeur d'usine.**
I was recently appointed Production Director.	**J'ai été récemment nommé(e) directeur de la production.**
I'm due to retire next year.	**Je dois partir à la retraite l'année prochaine.**
I've stayed with the same company.	**Je suis resté(e) dans la même entreprise.**
I've worked for ... since 1988/ for 20 years.	**Je travaille pour ... depuis 1988/ depuis 20 ans.**
I joined the company 20 years ago.	**J'ai intégré la société il y a 20 ans.**
I've changed jobs often.	**J'ai souvent changé de travail.**

Company history

The company was founded in 1884.	**La société a été fondée en 1884.**
We set up the company in 1982.	**Nous avons créé la société en 1982.**
The company was first registered in 1982.	**La société a été enregistrée pour la première fois en 1982.**
We went public 2 years ago.	**Notre société s'est introduite en Bourse il y a deux ans.**
There was a takeover bid.	**Il y a eu une offre publique d'achat (O.P.A.).**
The company was taken over by Blaskins.	**L'entreprise a été reprise par Blaskins.**
Later we merged with ...	**Ensuite, nous avons fusionné avec ...**

NUMBERS, see page 17/DATES, see page 15

Introducing the product

product line	**la ligne de produits**
product attributes	**les qualités f du produit**
product features	**les caractéristiques f du produit**
product benefits	**les valeurs f du produit**
product advantages	**les avantages m du produit**

Our main product is ...	**Notre produit principal est ...**
We have two major product lines: ...	**Nous avons deux lignes de produits phares: ...**
It is designed to ...	**Il a été conçu pour ...**

Life & service

after sales/customer service	**le service après vente**
maintenance	**l'entretien m**
repairs	**la réparation**
replacement	**le remplacement**

It will last at least ten years.	**Il va durer au moins dix ans.**
It should be regularly serviced.	**Il devrait être régulièrement entretenu.**
We have a 24-hour help desk.	**Nous avons un service d'assistance 24 heures sur 24.**
Any repairs will be carried out on site.	**Toute réparation sera faite sur place.**

Delivery

You can expect delivery within 2 weeks.	**Vous pourrez être livré dans les deux semaines.**
The earliest delivery will be next month.	**La livraison la plus rapide sera le mois prochain.**
The delivery may be delayed by 24 hours.	**La livraison peut être retardée de 24 heures.**

Price

low/cheap	**bas(se)/bon marché**
medium/reasonable	**moyen(ne)/raisonnable**
high/expensive	**élevé(e)/cher (-ère)**

The product is reasonably-priced.	**Le produit a un prix raisonnable.**
We can offer you a 15% discount.	**Nous pouvons vous offrir une remise de 15%.**

CUSTOMER SERVICE, see page 66/PRODUCTS, see page 82

Introductions

Touring the premises

office building	**les bureaux** *m*
plant/factory	**l'usine** *f***/l'unité** *f* **de fabrication**
manufacturing centre/center	**l'unité de production**

Offices

board room	**la salle de conférences**
canteen	**la cantine**
corridor	**le couloir**
floors	**les étages** *m*
lift/elevator	**l'ascenseur** *m*
meeting room	**la salle de réunions**
open-plan design	**un aménagement de bureau ouvert**

Office furniture & equipment

desk	**le bureau**
fax machine	**le télécopieur/le fax**
filing cabinet	**le meuble de rangement**
PC	**le PC**
photocopier	**la photocopieuse**
printer	**l'imprimante** *f*

Plant layout

components	**les pièces détachées**
despatch/dispatch area	**la zone d'expédition**
factory floor	**les ateliers** *m*
machine room	**la salle des machines**
paint shop	**l'unité** *f* **de peinture**
raw materials	**les matières** *f* **premières**

Showing visitors around

I'm pleased to welcome you to …	**Je suis heureux (-euse) de vous accueillir à …**
Welcome to …	**Bienvenue à …**
Please come this way.	**Par là s'il vous plaît.**
Follow me.	**Suivez-moi.**
Be careful!	**Faites attention!**
Mind/Watch your head!	**Faites attention à votre tête!**
Over there, you can see …	**Là-bas, vous pouvez voir …**
Are there any questions?	**Y-a-t-il des questions?**

Communication Skills

BUSINESS PRESENTATIONS

Check-list

To help you organize your presentation, it is useful to plan it around the following stages:

1. The introduction	❑	**1. L'introduction**
2. The overview	❑	**2. Le sommaire**
3. The main part	❑	**3. La partie principale**
4. The summary	❑	**4. Le résumé**
5. The ending	❑	**5. La conclusion**
6. Questions and answers	❑	**6. Questions et réponses**

---

1. The introduction

Good morning/afternoon, ladies and gentlemen/colleagues.	**Bonjour mesdames, mesdemoiselles, messieurs/chers collègues.**
My name is …	**Je m'appelle …**
I work for Rossomon as Marketing Director.	**Je travaille pour Rossomon en tant que directeur marketing.**
I am the Personnel Director at Rossomon.	**Je suis le chef du personnel chez Rossomon.**
In this talk, I'd like to … describe the main activities of our company.	**Dans ce discours, j'aimerais … décrire les activités principales de notre société.**

INTRODUCTIONS, see page 23/COMPANY POSITIONS, see page 28

present our product range.	**présenter notre gamme de produits.**
explain the production processes at our plant.	**expliquer les différents procédés de production de notre usine.**

2. The overview

I've divided my talk into 4 main parts.	**J'ai divisé mon discours en 4 parties principales.**
My presentation is split into 4 major sections.	**Ma présentation est divisée en 4 parties principales.**
In the description, I aim to cover the 4 key processes.	**Dans la description, je souhaite couvrir les 4 procédés-clé.**
Firstly, we'll look at …	**Premièrement, nous verrons …**
Secondly, I'm going to talk about …	**Deuxièmement, je vous parlerai de …**
After that, I'll tell you about …	**Après cela, je vous parlerai de …**

The order of points

First(ly)	**Premièrement**
Second(ly)	**Deuxièmement**
Third(ly)	**Troisièmement**
Fourth(ly)	**Quatrièmement**
After that	**Après cela**
Next	**Ensuite**
Finally	**Finalement**

3. The main part

Now let's look at the first point.	**Voyons à présent le premier point.**
Now I'd like to start the first part.	**J'aimerais commencer à présent la première partie.**

Ending a point

That's all about …	**Ceci étant pour …**
That's all I want to say about the first point.	**C'est tout ce que je voulais dire sur le point numéro un.**

NUMBERS, see page 17

That brings me to the end of the first part.	**Ce qui m'amène à la fin de la première partie.**

Moving on to the next point

Next let's look at …	**Ensuite, voyons …**
Now I'd like to move on to the next point.	**À présent, j'aimerais poursuivre avec le point suivant.**
So now I'd like to talk about …	**Donc maintenant, j'aimerais parler de …**

Visual aids

As you can see on the transparency, …	**Comme vous pouvez le voir sur le transparent, …**
You can see the relevant information …	**Vous pouvez voir les données pertinentes …**
on the screen	**à l'écran** *m*
on the transparency	**sur le transparent**
in the illustration	**sur l'illustration** *f*
in the drawing	**dans le dessin**
from the model	**sur le modèle**
from the plan	**sur le plan**

The relevant figures are shown …
__Les données pertinentes sont montrées …__

on the pie/bar chart	by a solid/broken/dotted line
dans le camembert/ l'histogramme *m*	**par un tracé continu/discontinu/ en pointillés**

The shaded boxes …	**Les parties** *f* **colorées …**
The unshaded circles …	**Les cercles** *m* **qui ne sont pas colorés …**
The blue triangles …	**Les triangles** *m* **bleus …**
The red rectangles …	**Les rectangles** *m* **rouges …**
show the major activities.	**représentent les activités principales.**

COLOURS/COLORS, see page 36

Colours/Colors

black	**noir(e)**	orange	**orange**
blue	**bleu(e)**	pink	**rose**
brown	**brun(e)**	purple	**violet(te)**
dark	**foncé(e)**	red	**rouge**
green	**vert(e)**	silver	**argenté(e)**
grey/gray	**gris(e)**	white	**blanc(he)**
light	**clair(e)**	yellow	**jaune**

4. The summary

Well, that brings me to the end of my final point.	**Bien, c'est ce qui m'amène à la fin de mon dernier point.**
That concludes the main part of my talk.	**Ceci conclue la partie principale de ma présentation.**
So now, I'd just like to summarize the main points.	**À présent, je voudrais résumer les points essentiels.**
In brief, we have looked at …	**En résumé, nous avons vu que …**

5. The ending

That's all I have to say for now.	**C'est tout ce que j'avais à dire pour l'instant.**
I hope that …	**J'espère que …**
the presentation has given you all the relevant information for your needs.	**cette présentation vous a donné les informations pertinentes pour vos besoins.**
the description has provided you with a clear picture of our activities.	**cette description vous a fourni un regard plus clair sur nos activités.**

6. Questions and answers

Are there any questions?	**Y-a-t-il des questions?**
Your question, please.	**Votre question, s'il vous plaît.**
Any more questions?	**D'autres questions?**
Does that answer your question?	**Ceci répond-il à votre question?**
If there are no more questions, I'd like to thank you for your attention.	**S'il n'y a plus de questions, je voudrais vous remercier pour votre attention.**

MEETINGS, CONFERENCES AND TRADE FAIRS

Preparing for the meeting

the chairperson	**le président**
the participants	**les participants** *m*
an agenda	**un ordre du jour**
a secretary	**une secrétaire**
the minutes	**les notes** *f*
point	**le point**
item	**la question (à l'ordre du jour)**
AOB (any other business)	**autres matières à l'ordre du jour**
to prepare	**préparer**
to draft	**rédiger**
to circulate	**faire circuler**

Arranging the time and place

I'd like to call a meeting to discuss …	**Je voudrais solliciter une réunion afin de discuter de …**
I'd like to fix a time and place for the meeting.	**Je voudrais fixer une heure et un lieu pour la réunion.**
Does Monday at … o'clock suit you?	**Lundi à … vous convient-il?**
We are planning to meet in my office/the meeting room.	**Nous avons l'intention de nous réunir dans mon bureau/la salle de réunion.**

Preparing the agenda

I've prepared an outline agenda.	**J'ai préparé un ordre du jour schématique.**
Could you look through it, please?	**Pourriez-vous y jeter un œil, s'il vous plaît?**
Could you add any points you'd like to discuss?	**Pourriez-vous rajouter les points dont vous aimeriez débattre?**
Could I ask you to lead item 2 on staff training?	**Pourrais-je vous demander de mener le point numéro 2 sur la formation?**
I've finalized the agenda.	**J'ai terminé l'ordre du jour.**
You'll receive all the papers tomorrow.	**Vous recevrez tous les documents demain.**

ARRANGING APPOINTMENTS, see page 12/TIME, see page 16

COMMUNICATION SKILLS

Meetings, conferences and trade fairs

The Chairperson's role

Opening the meeting

Good morning/afternoon, ladies and gentlemen/colleagues.	**Bonjour, mesdames, messieurs/chers collègues.**
If we are all here … let's start./shall we start?	**Si nous sommes tous présents, … commençons./pouvons-nous commencer?**
First of all I'd like to introduce …	**Tout d'abord j'aimerais vous présenter …**
Would you like to say a few words about yourselves?	**Voudriez-vous dire un mot sur vous-mêmes?**
Have you all got a copy of the agenda?	**Avez-vous tous reçu une copie de l'ordre du jour?**
The objective/purpose/aim/target of this meeting is to …	**L'objectif** m **/La raison/L'objet** m **/Le but de cette réunion est de …**
Now let's look at the agenda in detail.	**À présent, passons en revue l'ordre du jour.**
As you can see there are four main points/items.	**Comme vous pouvez le constater, il y a 4 points essentiels/questions essentielles.**
I think we will need about 30 minutes for point/item 1, 20 minutes for point/item 2, …	**Je pense qu'il nous faudra environ 30 minutes pour le point numéro un/la question une, 20 minutes pour le point numéro 2/la question 2, …**
We will break for coffee/lunch at …	**Nous ferons une pause café/une pause pour le déjeuner à …**
We aim to finish at … o'clock.	**Nous avons l'intention de terminer à … heures.**
Is that OK for everybody?	**Cela convient-il à tout le monde?**

Moving to points on the agenda

Let's look at the first point.	**Regardons le point numéro un.**
I'd like to start with item one.	**Je voudrais commencer avec la question une.**
OK, Marianne, over to you.	**O.K., Marianne, à vous.**
I believe you're going to lead this one.	**Je pense que vous allez mener ce point-ci.**

Can I ask you to present the background information?	**Puis-je vous demander de nous présenter les informations complémentaires?**
Right. Let's move on to the next point.	**Bien. Passons au point suivant.**
Aziz, would you like to introduce the next point?	**Aziz, voulez-vous introduire le point suivant?**
OK, on to item 2.	**O.K., à la question 2.**

Keeping the meeting on track

Inviting contributions

What's your opinion on this, Liz.	**Quelle est votre opinion là-dessus, Liz?**
Henri, we haven't heard from you yet.	**Henri, nous ne vous avons pas encore entendu.**
Would you like to add anything, Rafael?	**Voudriez-vous ajouter quelque chose, Rafael?**

Stopping people talking

We can't all speak at once. David first, then Liz, then Henri.	**Nous ne pouvons pas parler tous en même temps. D'abord David, puis Liz, puis Henri.**
One at a time, please!	**Un à la fois, s'il vous plaît!**
Well, thank you, Rafael. I think that's clear now. Could we have some other opinions?	**Bien, merci, Rafael. Je pense que c'est clair à présent. Y a-t-il d'autres remarques?**

Dealing with problems of comprehension

I'm sorry. I didn't hear what you said. Would you mind repeating it, please?	**Je suis désolé(e). Je n'ai pas entendu ce que vous avez dit. Pourriez-vous répéter, s'il vous plaît?**
I'm sorry. I don't quite follow you.	**Je suis désolé(e). Je ne vous suis pas tout à fait.**
Could you go over that again, please?	**Pourriez-vous reprendre ce point, s'il vous plaît?**
What exactly do you mean by …?	**Que voulez-vous dire exactement par …?**

Preventing irrelevance

I'm afraid that's outside the scope of this meeting.	**Je crains que cela n'entre plus dans les limites de cette réunion.**
We're beginning to lose sight of the main point.	**Nous sommes en train de perdre de vue le point essentiel.**
Keep to the point, please.	**Restez dans les limites du sujet, s'il vous plaît.**
We're running short of time.	**Il ne nous reste plus tellement de temps.**
Please be brief.	**Soyez bref, s'il vous plaît.**

Paraphrasing

So what you're saying is …	**Donc, ce que vous dîtes, c'est …**
In other words …	**En d'autres termes …**
So you mean …	**Donc, vous pensez …**

Controlling decision-making

I'd like to (formally) propose that …	**Je voudrais vous proposer (formellement) de …**
Can we take a vote on that proposal?	**Pouvons-nous voter sur cette proposition?**
All those in favour/favor. Right. All those against. Right, thank you.	**Tous ceux-ci pour. Bien. Tous ceux-là contre. Bien, merci.**
So that motion has been accepted/rejected by 4 votes to 3.	**Donc cette proposition a été acceptée/rejetée par 4 votes contre 3.**

Summarizing & minuting/recording

To sum up then, …	**Donc, pour résumer, …**
So far we have agreed that …	**Jusqu'à présent, nous étions d'accord que …**
Could you minute/record that, please?	**Pourriez-vous prendre note de cela, s'il vous plaît?**
Have you minuted/recorded that?	**Avez-vous noté cela?**

Concluding a point on the agenda

So, on point one we have agreed that …	**Alors, dans le point numéro un, nous avons convenu que …**

NUMBERS, see page 17

That leaves two follow-up tasks.	**Ce qui laisse deux tâches/ missions complémentaires.**
Paul, could you prepare some information for the next meeting?	**Paul, pourriez-vous nous préparer des informations pour la prochaine réunion?**
Henri, when could we have the results of your survey?	**Henri, quand pourrons-nous avoir les résultats de votre étude?**
Well, I think that covers everything on that point.	**Bien, je pense que nous avons passé en revue ce point.**

Closing the meeting

Right. That just about covers everything.	**Bien, ceci couvre tout le sujet.**
So, the next meeting will be on … (*date*) at … (*time*)	**Donc, la prochaine réunion sera le … à …**
I'll circulate the minutes of this meeting in the next few days.	**Je ferai circuler les notes/le rapport de cette réunion dans les prochains jours.**
Thanks for your participation.	**Merci pour votre participation.**
Right, I declare the meeting closed.	**Bien, je déclare cette réunion terminée.**

The Participants' role

Getting the chair's attention

(Mister/Madam) chairman.	**Monsieur/Madame le Président.**
Excuse me for interrupting.	**Excusez-moi de vous interrompre.**
May I come in here?	**Puis-je intervenir à ce sujet?**
I'd like to comment on that.	**Je voudrais commenter ce point.**

Giving opinions

strongly

I'm convinced/sure/positive that …	**Je suis convaincu(e)/sûr(e)/ certain(e) que …**
I strongly believe that …	**Je crois fortement que …**
I definitely/certainly think that …	**Je pense de façon catégorique/ certaine que …**

neutrally

I think/consider/feel that ...	Je pense/considère/sens que ...
As I see it, ...	La façon dont moi, je le vois, ...
From my point of view ...	De mon point de vue ...

weakly

I'm inclined to think that ...	Je suis enclin(e) à croire que ...
I tend to think that ...	J'ai tendance à penser que ...

Making recommendations

Shall we hear the figures now?	Voulez-vous entendre les chiffres à présent?
Let's discuss the results first.	Discutons d'abord des résultats.
I suggest we postpone the decision till the next meeting.	Je suggère que nous remettions la décision à la prochaine réunion.

Agreeing or disagreeing with others

Full agreement

I totally agree with you.	Je suis entièrement d'accord avec vous.
I'm in total agreement with you on that point.	Je suis en parfait accord avec vous sur ce point.
I'm all in favour/favor of that proposal.	Je suis tout à fait en faveur de cette proposition.

Partial agreement

Up to a point, I agree with you, but ...	Jusqu'à un point, je suis d'accord avec vous, mais ...
Of course, on the other hand ...	Bien entendu, par contre ...
You could/may be right, but ...	Vous avez peut-être raison, mais ...

Disagreement

I don't agree with you on that point.	Je ne suis pas d'accord avec vous sur ce point.
I can't accept that proposal.	Je ne peux pas accepter cette proposition.
I disagree totally.	Je ne suis pas du tout d'accord.

CONFERENCES

congress	**le congrès**
symposium	**le colloque**
seminar	**le séminaire**
convention	**la convention**
to attend	**assister**
to participate	**participer**
chairperson	**le président**
participant	**le participant**
delegate	**le délégué**
speaker	**l'intervenant** *m*
keynote speaker	**le premier intervenant**
presenter	**le présentateur**

Introducing the speaker

It gives me great pleasure to introduce Dr Alfred Bermann.
J'ai le grand plaisir de vous présenter le Dr Alfred Bermann.

I am very pleased to present Professor Martina Meier.
Je suis très heureux (-euse) de vous présenter le Professeur Martina Meier.

He is going to present the findings of his latest research.
Il va nous présenter les résultats de ses dernières recherches.

She will deliver a paper entitled 'Management 2000'.
Elle va nous remettre un rapport intitulé «Management 2000».

Research and findings

findings	**les découvertes** *f*
results	**les résultats** *m*
conclusions	**les conclusions** *f*
outcome	**l'issue** *f*

Addressing the audience

Ladies and gentlemen
Mesdames, Messieurs

Dear colleagues
Chers collègues

It gives me great pleasure to address you today on …
J'ai le plaisir de prendre la parole aujourd'hui au sujet de …

I should also like to thank … for sponsoring me.
Je devrais aussi remercier … de m'avoir parrainé.

INTRODUCTIONS, see page 23

Thanking the speaker & inviting questions

I should like to thank Dr Alfred Bermann for his most interesting talk.	Je voudrais remercier le Dr Alfred Bermann pour sa très intéressante intervention.
Dr Bermann's talk touched many important issues.	L'intervention du Dr Bermann a soulevé de nombreux problèmes importants.
So now, there will be an opportunity for questions.	Bien, maintenant vous avez l'occasion de poser des questions.
Are there any questions or comments?	Y-a-t-il des questions ou des commentaires?
Yes, your question, please.	Oui, votre question, s'il vous plaît.

Concluding the talk

I'm afraid that I will have to interrupt this interesting discussion.	Je crains d'être obligé(e) d'interrompre cette discussion intéressante.
It is now time to move on to the next speaker.	A présent il est temps de poursuivre avec le prochain intervenant.
We have scheduled a lunch break/coffee break until ... o'clock.	Nous avons prévu une pause pour le déjeuner/une pause café jusqu'à ... heures.
The next talk will start at ... o'clock.	La prochaine intervention débutera à ... heures.

Concluding the conference

It has been a very interesting conference.	Cela a été une conférence très intéressante.
We have heard a range of stimulating presentations.	Nous avons entendu une série de présentations encourageantes.

It has been ...
  inspiring
  stimulating
  intriguing
  provocative
	Cela a été ...
	  enrichissant
	  encourageant
	  fascinant
	  provocant

Finally, we look forward to seeing you all again next year in Miami.	Pour finir, nous espèrons vous revoir tous l'année prochaine à Miami.

QUESTIONS AND ANSWERS, see page 36

Exhibitions and Trade Fairs

The Exhibitor's role

Introducing yourself and your company

Good morning/afternoon. My name's …	**Bonjour. Je m'appelle …**
Here's my card.	**Voici ma carte.**
Do you know our company?	**Connaissez-vous notre société?**
I'm sure you know our organization.	**Je suis sûr(e) que vous connaissez notre organisme.**
We make/provide …	**Nous faisons/fournissons …**
We are the largest company in our field.	**Nous sommes la plus importante société dans notre domaine.**

Finding out about your visitor

What do you do?	**Que faites-vous?**
Who do you work for?	**Pour qui travaillez-vous?**
What do they do?	**Que font-ils?**
Would you like some information about our products/services?	**Souhaiteriez-vous des informations sur nos produits/services?**
Any specific product/service?	**Un produit/service spécifique?**
What exactly would you like to know?	**Que désireriez-vous savoir exactement?**

Giving information to the visitor

We have a number of products which can …	**Nous avons un certain nombre de produits qui peuvent …**
For your needs, I would recommend …	**Pour vos besoins, je conseillerais …**
This product/service …	**Ce produit/service …**
is just right for your needs.	**est parfaitement adapté à vos besoins.**
exactly covers your needs.	**couvre exactement vos besoins.**
could be the answer.	**pourrait être la réponse.**
may be able to solve your problem.	**pourrait être capable de résoudre votre problème.**

GREETINGS, see page 23/INTRODUCING THE COMPANY, see page 28

I'm afraid we don't make anything like that.	Je regrette, mais nous faisons rien s'y rapportant.
I'm sorry but we can't provide that service.	Je suis désolé(e), mais nous ne pouvons assurer un tel service.
Please take a copy of our brochure/leaflet/prospectus.	S'il vous plaît, prenez un exemplaire de notre brochure/plaquette/prospectus.
It contains all the product information.	Il/Elle contient toutes les informations sur nos produits.

Planning follow-up action

Would you like ...	Souhaiteriez-vous ...
someone to visit your company?	que quelqu'un se rendre à votre société?
us to prepare a quotation?	que nous préparions un devis?
to discuss this over lunch/dinner/a coffee?	que nous en discutions pendant le déjeuner/le dîner/autour d'un café?
to return to the stand/booth later?	revenir au stand plus tard?
a demonstration of the equipment?	une démonstration du matériel?
I/We'd be delighted to ...	Je serais/Nous serions heureux (-euse) de ...
visit your company	visiter votre société
prepare a quotation	préparer un devis
discuss this later	d'en discuter plus tard

Saying goodbye

| We'll be in touch with you next week/month. | Nous vous recontacterons la semaine prochaine/le mois prochain. |
| Good-bye. | Au-revoir. |

The Visitor's role

Explaining your areas of interest

| I am interested in ... | Je suis intéressé(e) par ... |
| I'm in the ... field. | Je suis dans le domaine ... |

INTRODUCING THE PRODUCT, see page 31

I would like to know more about …	Je voudrais en savoir plus sur …

Questioning the exhibitor

Could you explain exactly …	Pourriez-vous m'expliquer exactement …
what this product does?	ce que fait ce produit?
how this machine works?	comment cette machine fonctionne?
where this service is provided?	où ce service est assuré?
if this service is available here?	si ce service est disponible ici?

Planning follow-up action

I/We would like …	Je voudrais/Nous voudrions …
someone to visit our company.	que quelqu'un se rende à notre société.
to have a quotation.	avoir un devis.
to discuss this further.	en discuter plus tard.
to see a demonstration.	voir une démonstration.
I look forward to hearing from you.	Dans l'attente de vos nouvelles.

Communication difficulties

Could you speak …	Pourriez-vous parler …
a bit slower, please?	plus lentement, s'il vous plaît?
a bit louder, please?	plus fort, s'il vous plaît?
I'm sorry, could you repeat that, please?	Je suis désolé(e), pourriez-vous répéter, s'il vous plaît?
What exactly do you mean by …?	Que voulez-vous dire exactement par …?
Could you explain that, please?	Pourriez-vous m'expliquer cela, s'il vous plaît?

Showing understanding

I see.	Je vois.
I understand.	Je comprends.
Yes, I've got that now.	Oui, j'ai compris cela maintenant.
Yes, that's clear now.	Oui, c'est clair à présent.

COMMUNICATION SKILLS

NEGOTIATIONS

The focal part of most negotiations is the contract, which plays a central role in French business life. It is generally very detailed, with a multitude of clauses to cover any eventuality.

Check-list

To help you prepare your negotiation, it is useful to plan it around the following stages:

1. Creating the right environment	❑	1. **Créer le milieu approprié**
2. Defining the issues	❑	2. **Définir les problèmes**
3. Establishing opening positions	❑	3. **Etablir des positions d'ouverture**
4. Handling the offer and counter-offer	❑	4. **Traiter la proposition et la contre-proposition**
5. Testing the other side's case	❑	5. **Tester la position de l'autre**
6. Strengthening your case	❑	6. **Renforcer votre position**
7. Handling stalemate	❑	7. **Traiter une impasse**
8. Clinching the deal	❑	8. **Conclure le marché**
9. Getting it in writing	❑	9. **Mettre le contrat par écrit**
10. The legal aspects	❑	10. **Les aspects juridiques**

The processes

to negotiate	**négocier**
to bargain	**entrer en négociations**
to discuss	**discuter**
to persuade	**persuader**
to compromise	**trouver un compromis**
to make a deal	**proposer un marché**
to strike a bargain	**conclure une affaire**
to reach agreement	**trouver un accord**
to draft a contract	**rédiger un contrat**
to sign the contract	**signer le contrat**
to implement the agreement	**rendre effectif le contrat**
to break the contract	**rompre le contrat**

Negotiations

The subject of negotiation

price	**le prix**
delivery and terms	**livraison** f **et conditions** f
payment and credit	**le paiement et le crédit**
discount	**la remise** f
licences/licenses	**les autorisations** f
warranties and guarantees	**les garanties** f **et cautions** f
penalties	**les pénalités** f
legal jurisdiction	**la juridiction**

1. Creating the right environment

For key phrases for introducing yourself and making small talk, see Section 1 Making Contact: Introductions and Socializing.

2. Defining the issues

Stating the agenda

OK. Shall we start?	**Bien, commençons-nous?**
Our position is as follows:	**Notre position est la suivante:**
We would like to buy ...	**Nous souhaiterions acheter ...**
We are interested in selling ...	**Nous sommes intéressés par la vente ...**
We need to reach agreement about ...	**Nous devons trouver un accord sur ...**
We are eager to make a decision about ...	**Nous sommes impatients de décider de ...**
The aim/purpose/target/objective of this negotiation is to solve the problem over ...	**L'objet/La raison/Le but/L'objectif de cette négociation est de résoudre le problème de ...**

Clarifying the agenda

So, if we understand you correctly, you want to sell ...	**Donc, si nous vous comprenons bien, vous désirez vendre ...**
So, are we right in thinking that you would like us to sell ...?	**Donc, avons-nous raison de penser que vous désirez que nous vendions ...?**

INTRODUCTIONS, see page 23/SOCIALIZING, see page 25

We fully understand your views/position …	Nous comprenons entièrement votre point de vue/position …
but what would you actually like us to do?	mais que désirez-vous que nous fassions réellement?
but what precisely are you offering?	mais que nous offrez-vous précisément?

3. Establishing opening positions

Price

In your proposal, …	Dans votre proposition,
your asking price is …	le prix que vous souhaitez est de …
you have set the price at …	vous avez fixé le prix à …
We are willing to pay …	Nous sommes prêts à payer …
Our initial offer is …	Notre offre initiale est de …

Delivery and terms

In addition, we/you can deliver the goods on 25th July.	De plus, nous pouvons/vous pouvez livrer la marchandise le 25 juillet.
we can supply the products by 25th July.	nous pouvons fournir les produits avant le 25 juillet.
Our position is that we need the goods by 20th July.	En ce qui nous concerne, il nous faut la marchandise avant le 20 juillet.
Can you arrange delivery to our site by truck?	Pouvez-vous assurer la livraison en camion vers notre site?
However, you expect us to provide transport and insurance.	Néanmoins, vous attendez que nous prenions en charge le transport et l'assurance.
However, you do not agree to pay for …	Néanmoins, vous n'êtes pas d'accord pour payer le …

Payment and credit

We expect payment by bank transfer …	Nous demandons un paiement …
within 60 days.	à 60 jours par virement bancaire.
90 days after invoice.	90 jours après facturation.
90 days after order.	90 jours après la commande.

PAYMENT, see page 76/DISTRIBUTION, see page 71

Our normal payment terms are by letter of credit.	**Nos conditions de paiement habituelles sont une lettre de change.**
Do you accept our payment terms?	**Acceptez-vous nos conditions de paiement?**
We do not normally pay …	**Nous n'avons pas l'habitude de payer …**
in cash	**au comptant**
by bank transfer	**par virement bancaire**

Discount

However, we can offer an initial discount of 5%.	**Néanmoins, nous pouvons accorder une première remise de 5%.**
But we are prepared to reduce the total price by 5%.	**Mais nous sommes prêts à réduire le prix total de 5%.**
What discount can you offer?	**Quelle remise offrez-vous?**

Licences/Licenses

What licence/license can you offer?	**Quelle autorisation pouvez-vous offrir?**
We are prepared to offer a licence/license to sell the product.	**Nous sommes prêts à offrir une licence pour vendre le produit.**
We cannot grant a licence/license to manufacture the product.	**Nous ne pouvons accorder d'autorisation/de licence pour fabriquer ce produit.**
The licence/license will initially be limited to 5 years.	**L'autorisation/La licence va être limitée, dans un premier temps, à 5 ans.**

Warranties and guarantees

What warranties and guarantees do you offer?	**Quelles garanties et cautions offrez-vous?**
We warrant the goods for a period of 5 years.	**Nous garantissons la marchandise pour une période de 5 ans.**
We cover all parts and labour/labor for 1 year.	**Nous garantissons les pièces et la main d'œuvre pour une période d'un an.**

PRICING, see page 84/DATES, see page 15

COMMUNICATION SKILLS

Negotiations

In that case, we …	Dans ce cas, nous …
will replace the goods.	échangerons la marchandise.
repair the equipment free of charge.	réparerons le matériel gratuitement.
We cannot guarantee the goods against …	Nous ne pouvons pas garantir la marchandise en cas …
breakdown	de défaillance
normal wear and tear	d'usure normale

Penalties

What happens if anything goes wrong?	Qu'advient-il en cas de problème?
What compensation will you pay if …?	Quel dédommagement accorderez-vous, si …
We will claim compensation if …	Nous exigerons un dédommagement, si …
you don't deliver on time.	vous ne livrez pas à temps.
the goods are delayed.	la marchandise est retardée.
the equipment breaks down.	le matériel tombe en panne.

Legal jurisdiction

What happens if there is a dispute?	Qu'advient-il s'il y a un litige?
Any disputes will be settled according to French law.	Tout litige sera réglé selon la Loi française.
We resolve any disagreements by arbitration.	Nous réglons tout désaccord par arbitrage.

4. Handling the offer and counter-offer

Positive

That's great.	C'est génial.
(That's a) good/excellent/great idea.	C'est une bonne/excellente idée/une idée géniale.
We accept/agree.	Nous acceptons/Nous sommes d'accord.
We can accept your payment/delivery/discount terms.	Nous pouvons accepter vos conditions de paiement/livraison/remise.

LEGAL DEPARTMENT, see page 78/CONTRACT LAW, see page 121

Partial

Yes, but ...	**Oui, mais ...**
We're on the right track.	**Nous sommes sur le bon chemin.**
We're getting there.	**Nous avançons.**

Negative

That's unacceptable.	**C'est inacceptable.**
That's out of the question.	**C'est hors de question.**
We can't accept that.	**Nous ne pouvons accepter cela.**
We don't agree to that.	**Nous ne sommes pas d'accord avec cela.**
We are not in agreement over compensation clauses.	**Nous ne sommes pas d'accord avec les clauses de dédommagement.**

5. Testing the other side's case

Have you given us all the relevant facts?	**Nous avez-vous communiqué tous les faits pertinents?**
On what are those figures based?	**Sur quoi se basent ces chiffres?**

We have heard that ...
  your normal prices are ...
  normal delivery terms are ...
	**Nous avons appris que ...
	  vos prix habituels sont ...
	  conditions habituelles de livraison sont ...**

We don't follow the logic of your argument.	**Nous ne suivons pas la logique de votre argumentation.**
If your normal prices are ..., then we expect ...	**Si vos prix habituels sont ..., alors nous demandons ...**
Could you explain how you got to those figures?	**Pouvez-vous nous expliquer comment vous arrivez à ces chiffres?**

6. Strengthening your case

If we accept ...
  your prices, then we will have to raise our prices.
	**Si nous acceptons ...
	  vos prix, alors nous devrons augmenter les nôtres.**

That will not be good for our business.	**Ceci ne sera pas bon pour nos affaires.**

GIVING OPINIONS, see page 41

If you can reduce your price by ..., then we will ...	**Si vous pouvez baisser votre prix de ..., alors nous ...**
If you are prepared to speed up delivery, then we will ...	**Si vous êtes prêts à nous livrer plus rapidement, alors nous ...**
If you are willing to reconsider your payment terms, then we will ...	**Si vous êtes prêts à revoir vos conditions de paiement, alors nous ...**
look at prices for our next contract.	**réviserons nos prix lors de notre prochain contrat.**

7. Handling stalemate

We are very far apart on this issue.	**Nous sommes très loin de ce problème.**
Our positions are very different on the question of ...	**Notre position est très différente de la question de ...**
I don't think we can resolve this matter now.	**Je ne pense pas que nous puissions résoudre ce problème maintenant.**
Shall we summarise the points of agreement ...	**Résumons les points sur lesquels nous sommes d'accord ...**
and then take a short break.	**et faisons ensuite une petite pause.**
and then adjourn till this afternoon.	**et arrêtons-nous jusqu'à cet après-midi.**
So far, we've agreed on the following points: ...	**Jusqu'à présent, nous sommes tombés d'accord sur les points suivants ...**
We disagree on ...	**Nous ne sommes pas d'accord sur ...**
So we'll come back to those issues after the break.	**Donc nous reviendrons sur ces problèmes après la pause.**

8. Clinching the deal

We have covered a lot of ground in this meeting.	**Nous avons bien avancé lors de cette réunion.**
We cannot change our offer.	**Nous ne pouvons pas changer notre offre.**
This is our final offer.	**C'est notre offre définitive.**

We have/have not reached agreement on …	Nous sommes/ne sommes pas tombés d'accord sur …
You have accepted our terms on …	Vous avez accepté nos conditions de …
You cannot accept our terms on …	Vous ne pouvez accepter nos conditions de …
Let me go over all the details again.	Laissez-moi revenir sur tous les détails.
Have I covered everything?	Ai-je traité de tout?
Do you agree?	Êtes-vous d'accord?
Do you accept these terms?	Acceptez-vous ces conditions?

9. Getting it in writing

I will draft an outline agreement.	Je vais rédiger une ébauche de contrat.
Can you prepare a draft contract?	Pouvez-vous préparer un projet de contrat?
I will send the agreement to you for your comments.	Je vous ferai parvenir le contrat pour commentaires.
Please send the draft contract to me for our comments.	S'il vous plaît, faites-moi parvenir le projet de contrat pour commentaires.
After the contract/agreement has been signed, we can … make the goods. deliver the equipment.	Une fois que le contrat/l'accord m a été signé, nous pouvons … préparer la marchandise. livrer le matériel.

10. The legal aspects

contract	le contrat
parties to the contract	les parties f du contrat
to sign a contract	signer un contrat
signatories to the contract	les signataires m du contrat
scope of the contract	le champ d'application du contrat
terms of the contract	les conditions f du contrat
clauses of the contract	les clauses f du contrat
to break a contract	rompre un contrat
breach of contract	la rupture de contrat

CONTRACT LAW, see page 121/LEGAL JURISDICTION, see page 52

PROJECTS AND PERFORMANCE

Check-list

To help you manage your project better, it is useful to plan it around the following stages or milestones:

1. Defining objectives	❏	1. **Définir les objectifs**
2. Prioritizing and sequencing activities	❏	2. **Donner une priorité et ordonner les activités**
3. Allocating resources	❏	3. **Allouer des ressources**
4. Evaluating performance	❏	4. **Evaluer la performance**
5. Project completion	❏	5. **Achèvement du projet**

Project types

Company reorganisation	**la réorganisation de la société**
Company restructuring	**la restructuration de la société**
Automation project	**le projet d'automatisation**
IT project	**le projet informatique**
Cost control project	**le projet de contrôle des dépenses**
Manpower planning project	**le projet de planification de la main d'œuvre**
Quality project	**le projet de qualité**
Research project	**le projet de recherche**
Installation project	**le projet d'installation**
Construction project	**le projet de construction**
Product launch	**le projet de lancement du produit**

The project team

The team consists of a ...	**L'équipe consiste en ...**
We have appointed a ...	**Nous avons nommé ...**
project leader	**un chef de projet**
project supervisor	**un responsable de projet**
project manager	**un directeur(-trice) de projet**
project assistant	**un assistant(e) de projet**
project secretary	**un secrétaire de projet**

57

COMMUNICATION SKILLS

1. Defining objectives

What exactly do we want to achieve?	Que voulons-nous réaliser exactement?
How exactly are we going to achieve it?	Comment le réaliserons-nous exactement?
Is this project really necessary?	Ce projet est-il vraiment nécessaire?
The aims/objectives/goals/ targets of this project are to …	Les objets/Les objectifs/Les buts/ Les cibles de ce projet sont de …
In this project, we …	Dans ce projet, nous …
aim to …	visons à …
plan to …	projetons de …
mean to …	voulons …
propose to …	proposons de …
intend to …	avons l'intention de …
reorganize the company	réorganiser la société
increase output	augmenter la production
introduce new equipment	présenter un matériel nouveau
launch an updated product	lancer un produit actualisé

2. Prioritizing and sequencing activities

The stages

The project consists of 10 phases.	Le projet consiste en 10 phases.
The project will be divided into 10 stages/activities.	Ce projet sera divisé en 10 étapes/ activités.
At the end of each stage, there is a milestone.	Chaque fin de stage représente une étape importante.
The phases and milestones are shown on this project scheduler.	Les phases et étapes vous sont montrées sur ce programme de projet.
You can see the phases …	Vous pouvez voir les phases …
on the critical path analysis	grâce à l'analyse du chemin critique
on the flowchart	sur le diagramme
on the Gantt chart	sur le graphique

Questions about the schedule

When are we due to start the project?	Quand devons-nous commencer le projet?

VISUAL AIDS, see page 35

When will the first stage be finished?	**Quand la première phase sera-t-elle terminée?**
How long will the first activity take?	**Combien de temps la première activité prendra-t-elle?**
When do we plan to complete the whole project?	**Quand avons-nous l'intention de boucler l'ensemble du projet?**

Details about the schedule

The first stage will start on 25th July.	**La première phase débutera le 25 juillet.**
We will begin this activity on 25th July.	**Nous commencerons cette première activité le 25 juillet.**
This phase will take 3 weeks.	**Cette phase prendra 3 semaines.**
This stage will last until 4th August.	**Cette phase durera jusqu'au 4 août.**
The next stage will be to ...	**L'étape suivante sera de ...**
The whole project must be completed by 15th April.	**L'ensemble du projet devra être terminé le 15 août.**

Prioritizing

The most important activity is ...	**L'activité principale est ...**
The most critical activity is ...	**L'activité la plus critique est ...**
The key stages are ...	**Les phases-clé sont ...**
The major stages are ...	**Les phases essentielles sont ...**

Project activities

collecting the data	**relever les données** f
interpreting the data	**interpréter les données**
researching the market	**faire une étude de marché**
designing the prototype	**concevoir le prototype**
testing the prototype	**tester le prototype**
selecting the subcontractors	**sélectionner les sous-traitants** m
recruiting the workforce	**recruter la main d'œuvre**
subcontracting the manufacture of components	**sous-traiter la fabrication des pièces** f
producing the equipment	**produire le matériel**
choosing an advertising agency	**choisir une agence de publicité**
agreeing the promotion	**être d'accord sur la promotion**

DATES, see page 15

finalizing the launch date	**donner l'accord final sur la date de lancement**
building the foundations	**poser les fondations**
installing the equipment	**installer le matériel**
starting up the plant	**créer l'usine**
handing over the plant	**céder l'usine**

3. Allocating resources

Forecasting

I am sure/convinced that … we will need more time.	**Je suis sûr(e)/convaincu(e) que… nous aurons besoin de plus de temps.**
It is likely that … we will need more money.	**Il est probable que … nous aurons besoin de plus d'argent.**
We may … need more people.	**Nous pourrions … avoir besoin de plus de personnes.**
We are unlikely to … need more equipment.	**Nous n'aurons probablement pas … besoin de plus de matériel.**
We definitely/certainly won't need more materials.	**Nous n'aurons sûrement/certainement pas besoin de plus de matériaux.**

Time

How much time will we need?	**De combien de temps avons-nous besoin?**
How long do we have for the first stage?	**De combien de temps disposons-nous pour la première phase?**
We will need … more/less time than budgeted.	**Nous aurons besoin … de plus/moins de temps que prévu.**
a longer time for stage 1.	**d'une période plus longue pour la phase numéro 1.**
a shorter time for stage 2.	**d'une période plus courte pour la phase numéro 2.**
another 3 days for stage 3.	**de 3 jours supplémentaires pour la phase numéro 3.**

We need to complete this phase in spring/summer/autumn (fall)/ winter.	**Nous devons terminer cette étape au printemps/en été/en automne/en hiver.**

Budget

How much will it cost?	**Quel en sera le coût?**
What is the budget?	**Quel est le budget?**
We will need more money than allocated.	**Nous aurons besoin de plus d'argent que prévu.**
It will cost more than budgeted.	**Le coût sera plus élevé que prévu.**
We forecast it will cost another £5,000.	**Nous prévoyons que cela coûtera encore £5.000.**

People

How many people do we need?	**Combien de personnes nous faut-il?**
We don't have enough people.	**Nous n'avons pas assez de personnes.**
Should we use our people or can we subcontract some of the work out?	**Devrions-nous utiliser notre personnel ou pouvons-nous sous-traiter une partie?**
We will need to employ/hire some extra …	**Nous devrons embaucher/ recruter un nombre supérieur de/d' …**
operators	**opérateurs**
specialists	**spécialistes**
technicians	**techniciens**
workers	**ouvriers**
We plan to subcontract some of the work out.	**Nous avons l'intention de sous-traiter une partie du travail.**

Responsibilities

The project leader has overall responsibility for …	**Le chef de projet a entière responsabilité sur …**
The project supervisor is in charge of …	**Le responsable de projet est chargé de …**
The project manager will take care of …	**Le directeur de projet s'occupera de …**

COMPANY POSITIONS, see page 28

The project assistant is responsible for …	**L'assistant de projet est responsable de …**
The project secretary will support/assist the project leader.	**La secrétaire de projet soutiendra/ assistera le chef de projet.**
financial questions	**les questions d'ordre financier**
personnel matters	**les problèmes d'ordre personnel**
day-to-day administration	**une administration générale**
accommodation on site	**un logement sur place**
contracts with suppliers	**les contrats avec les fournisseurs**
dealing with contractors	**négocier avec les entrepreneurs**
buying in materials	**acheter les matériaux**
organizing transport	**organiser le transport**

Materials

What materials do we need?	**Quels matériaux nous faut-il?**
Do we have the necessary equipment?	**Avons-nous le matériel requis?**
We don't have enough materials/equipment.	**Nous n'avons pas suffisamment de matériaux/matériel.**
We can produce the materials in-house.	**Nous pouvons fabriquer les matériaux de façon interne.**
We need to buy in the materials.	**Nous devons acheter les matériaux.**
What equipment do we need to hire/lease/buy?	**Quel matériel devons-nous louer/ prendre en leasing/acheter?**

4. Evaluating performance

The project

How is the project going?	**Comment avance le projet?**
The project is on target.	**Le projet n'a pas de retard.**
We are ahead of schedule.	**Nous sommes au delà de nos prévisions.**
We are behind schedule.	**Nous ne sommes pas dans les temps.**
The costs are as forecast.	**Les coûts sont dans les prévisions.**
The costs are running above/ below budget.	**Les coûts sont inférieurs/ supérieurs au budget.**

We have had a cost overrun.	**Nous avons eu un dépassement de budget.**
We are facing some difficulties/ problems with ...	**Nous rencontrons quelques difficultés/problèmes quant ...**
the timing of the project.	**au délai prévu pour le projet.**
the financing of the project.	**au financement du projet.**
the manpower for the project.	**à la main d'œuvre du projet.**
We can't ...	**Nous ne pouvons pas ...**
recruit the right workers.	**recruter les bons ouvriers.**
We need to review the situation.	**Nous devons revoir la situation.**
We need to look again at ...	**Nous devons revoir ...**
the schedule	**le programme**
the budgets	**les budgets**
our manpower needs	**la main d'œuvre requise**
our material requirements	**le matériel requis**
We must control costs.	**Nous devons contrôler les coûts.**
We need to ...	**Nous devons ...**
lay off some of the workers.	**renvoyer certains ouvriers.**
fire the supervisor.	**congédier le responsable.**

Personal qualities

The project leader is ...	**Le chef de projet est ...**
efficient	**compétent**
effective	**efficace**
hard-working	**travailleur**
competent	**capable**
conscientious	**consciencieux**
ambitious	**ambitieux**
The project supervisor is ...	**Le responsable de projet est ...**
logical	**logique**
methodical	**méthodique**
analytical	**analytique**
rational	**rationnel**
calm	**calme**
inflexible	**inflexible**
good with facts and figures	**à l'aise dans les chiffres**
The project manager is ...	**Le directeur de projet est ...**
practical	**pratique**
energetic	**énergique**
dynamic	**dynamique**
single-minded	**fermé**

impatient	**impatient**
good at negotiating	**bon négociateur**
The project designer is ...	**Le concepteur de projet est ...**
creative	**créatif**
imaginative	**imaginatif**
unorthodox	**pas clair**
impractical	**sans esprit pratique**
The project assistant is ...	**L'assistant de projet est ...**
sympathetic	**compréhensif**
perceptive	**perceptif**
communicative	**communicatif, ouvert**
good at developing team relationships	**bon dans le travail d'équipe**

Business trends

to increase/to raise	**augmenter/accroître**
to put up/to step up	**faire monter/remonter**
We have increased the budget for stage one.	***Nous avons augmenter le budget pour la phase numéro un.***
an increase/a rise	**une augmentation/une croissance**
We have to budget for an increase in the cost of materials.	***Nous devons budgétiser l'augmentation de coût concernant les matériaux.***
to decrease/to cut	**diminuer/couper**
to reduce	**réduire**
We have decreased the budget for phase two.	***Nous avons diminué le budget pour l'étape numéro deux.***

dramatic(ally)	**(de façon) radicale**
vast(ly)	**infini(ment)**
huge(ly)	**(de manière) gigantesque**
enormous(ly)	**énorme (-ément)**
substantial(ly)	**(de façon) substantielle**
considerable (considerably)	**considérable(ment)**
significant(ly)	**(de manière) significative**
moderate(ly)	**modéré(ment)**
slightly	**légère(ment)**
a little	**un peu**

to fall/to drop	tomber/chuter
to go down/to slump	baisser/s'effondrer
The manpower costs have fallen.	*Les frais de main d'œuvre ont baissé.*
a fall/a drop	une baisse/une chute
a cut/a reduction	une diminution/une réduction
a collapse/a slump	un effondrement/un écroulement
We estimate there will be a decrease in the cost of materials.	*Nous estimons qu'il y aura une diminution de coûts concernant les matériaux.*
to hold ... stable	garder stable ...
to maintain ... at the same level	maintenir au même niveau ...
We have kept costs constant during the project.	*Nous avons gardé les coûts constants durant le projet.*
to remain constant	demeurer constant
to stay stable	rester stable

5. Project completion

We have finished the project.	Nous avons terminé le projet.
The project is complete.	Le projet est achevé.
The plant is operational.	L'usine est opérationnelle.
The product is ready for launch.	Le produit est prêt pour être lancé.
We are ready to ... start up the new equipment	Nous sommes prêts à ... démarrer le nouveau matériel
We have managed to ... increase output	Nous avons réussi à ... augmenter la production
Congratulations. We have completed the project successfully.	Félicitations. Nous avons terminé le projet avec succès.
Well done. You have achieved your aim/goal/target/objective.	Bien joué. Vous avez atteint votre objectif/but/cible/vos objectifs.
I'd like to thank the project team for their ... hard work during the project commitment dedication collaboration participation	J'aimerais remercier l'équipe de projet pour ... son travail durant le projet son engagement sa conscience sa collaboration sa participation

Company Departments

Administration	la Gestion	65
Customer Service	le Service Clients	66
Distribution	la Distribution	71
Finance	le Service Finances/le Département des Finances	73
Legal	le Service Juridique/le Département Juridique	78
Marketing	le Département Marketing	81
Personnel	le Service du Personnel	86
Production	le Service Production	91
Purchasing	le Service des Achats	94
Sales	le Service des Ventes	96

In French-speaking countries, marketing and sales activities usually come under the control of **le Service Commercial.**

ADMINISTRATION

Administrative staff

administrator	**l'administrateur (-trice)**
clerk	**l'employé(e)**
office manager	**le directeur de bureau**
personal assistant	**l'adjoint** m, **l'assistante** f
she's the personal assistant to the Managing Director/CEO	***elle est l'adjoint au/l'assistante du P.D.G.***
secretary	**la secrétaire**
typist	**la dactylo**

Information organization

archive	**les archives** f
we keep the old records in the archives	***nous avons gardé les vieux dossiers dans les archives***
file (n)/(v)	**le classeur/classer**
have you filed that letter?	***avez-vous classé cette lettre?***
filing cabinet	**le meuble de rangement**
sort	**trier**

CUSTOMER SERVICE

agent	l'agent *m*
he acts as agent for us in Australia	*il est notre agent en Australie*
busy	occupé(e)
buy	acheter
cater for/serve	satisfaire
we cater for/serve a wide range of customers	*nous satisfaisons une large clientèle*
custom	la clientèle
customer	le client
customize	faire sur mesure, personnaliser
all our products are customized	*tous nos produits sont faits sur mesure*
deal	le marché, l'affaire *f*
delay	le retard
we're sorry for the delay	*nous sommes désolés pour ce retard*
demand	la demande
we can't keep up with demand	*nous ne pouvons pas suivre la demande*
discontinue	cesser
I'm afraid this line has been discontinued	*je crains que nous n'ayons cessé cette ligne de produits*
exchange (n)/(v)	le change/échanger
exempt	exempté(e) de
these products are VAT/sales tax exempt	*ces produits sont exemptés de T.V.A.*
export (n)/(v)	l'export *m* /exporter
fetch/pick up	aller chercher
we'll fetch/pick up the order this afternoon	*nous irons chercher la commande cet après-midi*
file (n)	le fichier
we keep all our customers on file	*nous gardons tous nos clients sur fichier*
customer file	le fichier client
handle (v)	gérer
import (v)	importer
install	installer

DISTRIBUTION, see page 71

when would you like the equipment installed?	*quand voudriez-vous que nous installions le matériel?*
item	l'article *m*
the order consisted of four items	*la commande était composée de 4 articles*
label	l'étiquette *f*
off-peak periods	heures *f* creuses
off-peak tariffs are much lower	*les tarifs aux heures creuses sont beaucoup plus intéressants*
off-season	hors saison
paperwork	le travail administratif
there's a lot of paperwork to do	*il y a beaucoup de travail administratif à faire*
part-exchange	la reprise en compte
quality	la qualité
run out of	être à court de, manquer de
I'm afraid we've run out of those items	*je crains que nous ne soyons à court de ces articles*
scarce	rare
schedule (n)/(v)	le programme/programmer
we've scheduled delivery for the end of the month	*nous avons programmé la livraison pour la fin du mois*
service	le service
the service is slow	*le service est lent*
after-sales service	le service après-vente
service industry	les services *m*
tariff	le tarif
triplicate	3 exemplaires
the order form needs filling out in triplicate	*le bon de commande doit être rempli en trois exemplaires*

Negotiating

bargain (n)/(v)	une bonne affaire/négocier
barter	troquer
conditions of sale	les conditions de vente
our conditions of sale are printed on the back of the invoice	*nos conditions de vente sont imprimées au dos de la facture*
haggle	marchander

NEGOTIATIONS, see page 48

negotiate	**négocier**
negotiable	**négociable**
these terms are not negotiable	***ces conditions ne sont pas négociables***
negotiation	**la négociation**

Complaints

blame (n)	**la responsabilité**
claim	**la réclamation**
the customer has made a claim for damages	***le client a fait une réclamation pour des dégâts***
compensate	**indemniser**
damage	**les dégâts** *m*
the accident caused a lot of damage	***l'accident a provoqué beaucoup de dégâts***
damages	**les dommages et intérêts**
fault (n)	**la faute**
guarantee (n)	**la garantie**
the guarantee lasts a year	***la garantie dure un an***
hazard	**le risque**
insure	**assurer**
insurance claim	**le sinistre**
insurance cover	**la couverture, la protection**
insurance policy	**la police d'assurance**
does your policy cover this claim?	***votre assurance couvre-t-elle ce sinistre?***
insurance premium	**la prime d'assurance**
overdue	**en retard**
the delivery is overdue	***la livraison est en retard***
repair	**réparer**
spoil	**abîmer**
the goods were spoiled in transit	***la marchandise a été abîmée durant le transport***

Payment

credit	**le crédit**
credit note	**l'avoir** *m*
hire purchase	**la location-vente**
invoice (n)/(v)	**la facture/facturer**

PAYMENT, see also page 76

you'll be invoiced at the end of the month	*vous allez être facturé à la fin du mois*
lease (n)/(v)	le bail/prendre à bail
outright purchase	l'achat *m* comptant
over-charged	avoir payé un prix excessif
overpay	surpayer, trop payer
you've overpaid so we'll send you a credit note	*vous avez trop payé, donc nous vous enverrons un avoir*
pay	payer
pay by cheque/check	payer par chèque
pay in cash	payer comptant
payable	payable, exigible
this invoice is payable in 30 days	*cette facture est payable dans 30 jours*
payment	le paiement
we demand payment in advance	*nous demandons un paiement d'avance*
prepaid	payé d'avance
please enclose a prepaid envelope	*joignez s'il vous plaît une enveloppe timbrée*
rebate	la remise
settle	régler
could you settle the bill in advance?	*pourriez-vous régler la facture d'avance?*
statement	le bilan, l'état *m* des comptes
we will send you a monthly statement	*nous vous enverrons un état mensuel de vos comptes*

Orders

acknowledge	accuser réception de
the order was acknowledged on 30 June	*nous avons accusé réception de votre commande le 30 juin*
acknowledgment	le reçu
available	disponible
availability	la disponibilité
bring forward/move up	reporter
we'd like to bring forward/move up the delivery date	*nous aimerions reporter le délai de livraison*
bulk	gros
we offer 10% discount for bulk orders	*nous offrons une remise de 10% pour des commandes en gros*

in bulk	**en gros**
cancel	**annuler**
cancellation	**l'annulation** *f*
confirm	**confirmer**
could you please confirm your order in writing?	***pourriez-vous confirmer votre commande par écrit, s'il vous plaît?***
notify	**signaler**
we'll notify you of any delay	***nous vous signalerons tout retard***
offer	**l'offre** *f*
order	**la commande**
fulfil/fulfill an order	**honorer une commande**
on order	**en commande**
we've got 25 on order	***nous en avons 25 en commande***
back order	**la commande en souffrance**
place an order	**passer une commande**
are you ready to place an order?	***êtes-vous prêt à passer commande?***
postpone	**reporter**
I'm afraid we'll have to postpone our order	***je crains que nous ne soyons obligés de reporter notre commande***
quote	**faire un devis**
could you quote us for 500 units?	***pourriez-vous nous établir un devis pour 500 unités?***
quotation	**le devis**
how long is your quotation valid for?	***combien de temps votre devis est-il valable?***
ready	**prêt(e)**
receive	**réceptionner**
receipt	**le reçu**
could you let me have a receipt?	***pourriez-vous me transmettre un reçu?***
reorder	**passer une nouvelle commande**
repeat order (v)	**repasser commande**
shortage	**l'insuffisance** *f*, **le manque**
there's a severe shortage of stock	***il y a un manque de stock considérable***
in stock/out of stock	**en stock/épuisé(e)**

DISTRIBUTION

by boat/ferry/ship/tanker	**par bateau/ferry/navire/pétrolier**
by post/special delivery/airmail	**par courrier/livreur/avion**
by truck/van/train	**par camion/camionnette/train**
cargo	**la cargaison**
carriage/freight	**le transport**
the price includes carriage	*le transport est inclus dans le prix*
cif (cost, insurance and freight)	**caf**
crate	**le cageot**
deliver	**livrer**
delivery	**la livraison**
delivery note	**le bon de livraison**
there should be a delivery note with the invoice	*il devrait y avoir un bon de livraison avec la facture*
delivery time	**le délai de livraison**
28 days delivery time	*le délai de livraison est de 28 jours*
depot	**le dépôt**
dispatch (v)	**expédier**
distribute	**distribuer**
duty	**la taxe**
enclose	**ci-joint**
please find enclosed our price list	*veuillez trouver ci-joint notre liste de prix*
envelope	**l'enveloppe** f
f.o.b. (free on board)	**franco à bord**
forward	**acheminer**
could you forward the goods to the distributor?	*pourriez-vous acheminer la marchandise vers le distributeur?*
freight	**fret**
in transit	**en cours de route**
the order was lost in transit	*la marchandise a été perdue en cours de route*
lading, bill of	**le chargement, le connaissement**
load (v)	**charger**
the goods were loaded onto the trucks	*la marchandise a été chargée dans des camions*
mail (n)/(v)	**le courrier/expédier**

pack (v)	**emballer**
package	**l'emballage** *m*
pallet	**la palette**
ship (v)	**expédier, charger**
have you shipped the goods?	*avez-vous chargé la marchandise?*
shipment	**la cargaison, l'expédition** *f*
unload	**décharger**

Channels

branch	**la succursale**
there is a branch in every major town	*il existe une succursale dans chaque ville importante*
bottleneck	**le bouchon**
chain	**la chaîne (de distribution)**
this store is part of a chain	*ce magasin fait partie d'une chaîne*
channel	**le circuit**
our main distribution channel is via the wholesaler to the retailer	*notre principal circuit de distribution est du grossiste au détaillant*
consignment	**l'arrivage** *m*
we're expecting a consignment later today	*nous attendons un arrivage plus tard dans la journée*
dealer	**le négociant, la négociante**
department store	**un grand magasin**
direct export	**l'export** *m* **direct**
franchise	**la franchise**
middleman	**l'intermédiaire** *m*
network	**le réseau**
we're building a dealer network	*nous mettons en place un réseau de négociants*
quota	**le contingent**
retail (n)/(v)	**la vente au détail/vendre au détail**
retail outlet	**le magasin de détail**
retailer	**le détaillant**
scarce	**peu abondant(e), rare**
storage	**le stockage**
tariff	**le tarif**
warehouse	**l'entrepôt** *m*
wholesale	**le grossiste**

FINANCE

accounts	les comptes *m*
the monthly accounts show all the figures	**les comptes mensuels montrent l'ensemble des chiffres**
accountancy	la comptabilité
accountant	le comptable
acquire	acquérir
acquisition	l'acquisition *f*
advance (n)/(v)	l'avance *f* /avancer
allocate	allouer
backdate	antidater
the cheque/check was backdated	**le chèque a été antidaté**
black, in the	être créditeur
books, keep the	tenir les comptes
bookkeeper	l'aide-comptable *m*
borrow	emprunter
break even (v)	rentrer dans ses frais, atteindre le seuil de rentabilité
break-even point	le seuil de rentabilité
we've reached the break-even point	**nous avons atteint le seuil de rentabilité**
budget (n)/(v)	le budget/budgéter
we've budgeted for a loss	**nous avons budgété une perte**
capital	le capital
cash	l'argent *m* comptant
cheque/check	le chèque
cost	les charges *f*
fixed/variable/running	fixes/variables/courantes
credit	le crédit
currency	la devise
debt	la dette
debtor	le débiteur
deduct	déduire
defer	différer
the taxation can be deferred until next year	**la taxation peut être différée jusqu'à l'année prochaine**
due	dû (due)
earn	gagner
earnings	les gains *m*

BANKING, see page 115

annual earnings exceeded our forecast	*les gains annuels ont dépassé nos prévisions*
finance (n)/(v)	le financement/financer
they are willing to finance the project	*ils sont prêts à financer le projet*
funds	les fonds *m*
income	le revenu
interest	l'intérêt *m*
interest rate	le taux d'intérêt
interest rates were cut by ½%	*les taux d'intérêts ont été réduits de ½ %*
lend	prêter
lender	le prêteur, la prêteuse
loan	le prêt
overdraw	mettre un compte à découvert
overdraft	le découvert
our overdraft facility is £50,000	*notre découvert autorisé/notre facilité de caisse est de £50.000*
owe	devoir
petty cash	le fonds de caisse
profit	le bénéfice
profitable	rentable
profitability	la rentabilité
rate	le taux
recover	reprendre
red, in the	être à découvert, être dans le rouge
save (v)	économiser, épargner
savings	les économies *f*, l'épargne *f*
subsidize	subventionner
subsidy	la subvention

Investment

base rate	le taux de base
terms are 2% above base rate	*les conditions sont de 2% au-dessus du taux de base*
bond	le bon, le titre
broker	le courtier
our broker advised us to sell our shares	*mon courtier m'a conseillé de vendre mes parts*
dealer	le cambiste

FINANCIAL PROBLEMS, see page 80

debenture	l'obligation *f* avec garantie *f*
dividend	le dividende
they announced the same dividend as last year	*ils ont annoncé le même dividende que l'année dernière*
earnings per share	le bénéfice par action
equity	la participation financière
gross yield	le rendement brut
invest	investir
investment	l'investissement *m*
portfolio	le portefeuille
you should have some oil shares in your portfolio	*vous devriez avoir quelques actions pétrolières dans votre portefeuille*
portfolio management	la gestion du portefeuille
premium	la prime
securities	les valeurs *f* boursières
the securities market can be very volatile	*les valeurs boursières du marché peuvent être très fluctuantes*
share/stock	l'action *f*
shareholder/stockholder	l'actionnaire *m*

Financial statements

asset	l'actif *m*, le bien
current assets	l'actif disponible
fixed assets	les immobilisations *f*
intangible assets	les valeurs *f* immatérielles
audit	l'apurement *m* des comptes
the annual audit	l'apurement annuel des comptes
auditor	le commissaire aux comptes
balance sheet	le bilan
the balance sheet looks very sound	*le bilan semble très solide*
cash flow	la marge brute
negative cash flow	une marge brute déficitaire
debit	le débit
depreciate	amortir
these assets are depreciated over 3 years	*ces biens sont amortis en trois ans*
depreciation	l'amortissement *m*
expenditure	les dépenses *f*

expenses	les frais *m*
gearing	l'ajustement *m*
goodwill	le fonds de commerce
goodwill is included under intangible assets	*le fonds de commerce est inclus dans les valeurs immatérielles*
gross	brut(e)
gross margin	la marge brute
gross profit	le bénéfice brut
half-yearly results	les résultats *m* semestriels
inventory	l'inventaire *m*
ledger	le registre
sales/purchase ledger	le registre des ventes/des achats
liabilities	le passif
current liabilities	les dépenses *f* courantes
margin	la marge
overheads	les frais généraux
our overheads are too high	*nos frais généraux sont trop élevés*
profit and loss account/ income statement	le compte des pertes et profits
quarterly	trimestriel (-elle)
reserves	les réserves *f*
results	les résultats *m*
retained earnings	les bénéfices *m* non distribués
return	le revenu
return on investment	le rendement
turnover/sales	le chiffre d'affaires
annual turnover/sales has doubled over 5 years	*le chiffre d'affaires a doublé en 5 ans*
working capital	le fonds de roulement
write-off (n)/(v)	l'amortissement *m*/amortir
this asset has now been written off	*ce bien a maintenant été amorti*

Payment

bad debt	la créance douteuse
this invoice has been posted as a bad debt	*cette facture a été enregistrée en tant que créance douteuse*
bank draft/check	la traite bancaire
bank statement	le relevé bancaire

PAYMENT, see also page 68

blank cheque/check	le chèque en blanc
bounce	sans provision
the cheque/check bounced	*c'est un chèque sans provision*
convert (v)	convertir
credit (n)	le crédit
credit limit	la limite d'un crédit
credit rating	le taux de crédit
direct debit	le débit direct
demand (n)	la demande
discount	la remise *f*
factoring	le recouvrement de créances
invoice (n)/(v)	la facture/facturer
letter of credit	la lettre de crédit
we will pay by letter of credit	*nous paierons par lettre de crédit*
outstanding payment	l'impayé *m*
$4,500 is still outstanding	*$4.500 restent toujours impayés/en souffrance*

Tax

capital gains tax	l'impôt *m* sur les plus-values, le bénéfice
corporation tax	l'impôt sur les sociétés
declare	déclarer
tax declaration	la déclaration fiscale
income tax	l'impôt sur le revenu
taxable	imposable
is this purchase taxable?	*cette acquisition est-elle imposable?*
tax allowance	la réduction d'impôts
tax avoidance	l'annulation *f* d'impôts
tax deductible	déductible d'impôts
tax evasion	la fraude fiscale
tax loophole	la façon (légale) d'échapper au fisc
tax relief	l'abattement *m* fiscal
you can get tax relief	*vous pouvez bénéficier d'un abattement fiscal*
tax threshold	le seuil fiscal
value added tax *(sales tax)*	la taxe sur la valeur ajoutée (T.V.A.)

LEGAL

abide by	**se conformer à**
abuse (n)/(v)	**l'abus** *m*/**abuser**
abuse of power	**l'abus de pouvoir**
appeal (n)	**le recours**
arbitrate	**arbitrer**
arbitration	**l'arbitrage** *m*
the dispute has gone	***ce litige s'est terminé en***
to arbitration	***arbitrage***
bequest (n)/(v)	**le legs/léguer**
the property was left to her	***cette propriété lui a été léguée***
as a bequest	
bond	**la caution**
civil law	**le droit civil**
claim (n)/(v)	**la revendication/revendiquer**
they have a claim	***ils ont une revendication***
claimant	**le réclamant**
conflict of interest	**le conflit d'intérêts**
copyright	**les droits** *m* **d'auteur**
court	**le tribunal**
go to court	**aller devant le tribunal**
we're going to court	***nous allons devant le tribunal***
damages	**les indemnités** *f* /**les**
	dommages *m* **et intérêts** *m*
fee	**les honoraires** *m*
indemnify	**indemniser**
indemnity	**l'indemnité** *f*
infringe copyright	**transgresser les droits d'auteur**
infringement	**l'infraction** *f*
irrevocable letter of credit	**la lettre de crédit irrévocable**
judicial	**judiciaire**
jurisdiction	**la juridiction**
this contract comes under	***ce contrat est placé sous***
British jurisdiction	***juridiction britannique***
law	**la loi**
within/outside the law	**conforme à loi/hors la loi**
against the law	**contre la loi**
legal	**légal(e)**
legal department	**le service du contentieux**
liability	**la responsabilité**

CONTRACT LAW, see page 121/EMPLOYMENT LAW, see page 122

limited liability	la responsabilité limitée
litigant	le plaideur
party	la partie
third party	le tiers
patent	le brevet
file a patent application	remplir un formulaire de demande de brevet
penalty	la pénalité
penalty clause	la clause pénale
the contract included a penalty clause for late completion	le contrat inclut une clause pénale en cas d'exécution tardive
pledge (v)	donner parole
precedent	le précédent
there is no precedent for this decision	il n'existe pas de précédent pour cette décision
settlement	le règlement
settle out of court	régler (le litige) hors tribunal
sue	poursuivre en justice
we can sue them for non-payment	nous pouvons les poursuivre pour non-paiement
suit	la poursuite
tax loophole	la façon (légale) d'échapper au fisc
trademark	la marque
tribunal	le tribunal
unlawful/illegal	illégal(e)
waive	renoncer
the company decided to waive its usual fee in this case	la société a décidé de renoncer à ses honoraires habituels dans cette affaire

People

actuary	l'actuaire m/f
advocate	le défenseur
attorney/barrister	l'avocat(e)
bailiff/sheriff	l'huissier m
lawyer	le juriste
legal advisor	le conseiller juridique
solicitor	l'avoué m

Crimes

backhander/kickback	**le pot-de-vin**
break the law	**enfreindre la loi**
bribe	**corrompre**
bribery	**la corruption**
embezzle	**détourner (les fonds)**
he embezzled all the company's profits	*il a détourné tous les bénéfices de la société*
embezzlement	**le détournement de fonds**
extort	**extorquer**
extortion	**l'extorsion** *f*
fraud	**la fraude**
he was accused of fraud	*il a été accusé de fraude*
fraudulent	**frauduleux (-euse)**
misconduct	**la faute grave**
professional misconduct	**la faute professionnelle**
swindle (v)	**escroquer**

Financial problems

bankrupt	**failli(e)**
to go bankrupt	**faire faillite** *f*
bankruptcy	**la faillite**
debt	**la dette**
foreclose	**saisir**
the bank foreclosed on the property	*la banque a saisi la propriété*
foreclosure	**la saisie**
insolvent	**insolvable**
insolvency	**l'insolvabilité** *f*
liquidate	**liquider**
liquidation	**la liquidation**
the company has gone into liquidation	*la société a été mise en liquidation*
liquidator	**le liquidateur**
receiver	**l'administrateur judiciaire**
a receiver has been appointed to sell off the assets	*un administrateur judiciaire a été désigné pour vendre les biens*
receivership	**l'administration** *f* **judiciaire**

MARKETING

capture market share	**accaparer une part du marché**
cartel	**le cartel**
client	**le client**
compete	**concurrencer**
competition	**la concurrence**
competitor	**le concurrent**
competitive	**concurrentiel (-elle)**
competitive pricing	**des prix concurrentiels**
domestic market	**le marché national**
down-market	**bas de gamme**
end-user	**le consommateur**
we sell direct to the end-user	***nous vendons directement aux consommateurs***
exhibit	**exposer**
exhibition	**l'exposition** f
flop (n)	**l'échec** m
the launch was a complete flop	***le lancement de ce produit s'est terminé par un échec complet***
forecast (v)	**prévoir**
we forecast that we will become market leader next year	***nous prévoyons de détenir la plus grande part de marché l'année prochaine***
goodwill	**le fonds de commerce**
logo	**le logo(type)**
market (n)	**le marché**
market leader	**détenir la plus grande part de marché, être le leader sur le marché**
market niche	**le créneau**
they have found a profitable market niche	***ils ont trouvé un bon créneau***
market penetration	**la pénétration du marché**
market segmentation	**la segmentation du marché**
market share	**la part de marché**
mass-market	**le marché de masse**
outlet	**le point de vente**
we have a retail outlet in most major cities	***nous avons un magasin de détail/un point de vente dans chaque ville importante***

SALES DEPARTMENT, see page 96

resistance	la résistance
there is some price resistance	*il existe une résistance au prix*
saturate	**saturer**
sector	**le secteur**
segment	**le segment**
share (n)/(v)	**la part/partager**
survey (n)	**l'étude *f* de marché**
target (n)/(v)	**le but/prendre pour but, viser**
up-market	**haut de gamme**
it's an upmarket product	*c'est un produit haut de gamme*
aimed at the luxury sector	*qui vise une clientèle de luxe*

Products

benefit (n)/(v)	**le bénéfice/bénéficier**
brand	**la marque**
brand leader	**le leader/numéro un de la marque**
brand loyalty	**la fidélité à la marque**
brand loyalty will stop	*la fidélité à la marque*
customers switching to	*empêchera les clients de passer*
generic products	*à des produits vendus sous*
	d'autres marques
by-product	**le sous-produit**
diversify	**diversifier**
feature (n)	**la caractéristique**
flagship	**la vedette**
a flagship product	*un produit vedette*
generic	**générique**
giveaway	**le cadeau promotionnel**
goods	**la marchandise**
label	**l'étiquette *f***
private label products are	*les produits à étiquette définie*
selling well	*se vendent mieux*
launch (v)	**lancer**
life cycle	**la durée de vie**
positioning	**le positionnement**
product line/range	**la ligne/la gamme de produit**
seasonal	**saisonnier (-ière)**
sell-by date	**la date limite de vente**
this product has passed its	*ce produit a dépassé sa date*
sell-by date	*limite de vente*

INTRODUCING THE PRODUCT, see page 31

shelf-life	la durée de conservation
tailor-made	sur mesure
trade mark	la marque de fabrique
white goods	l'électroménager *f*

Advertising

account executive	le responsable de la publicité
advertise	annoncer, faire de la publicité
advertisement	l'annonce *f*, la publicité
art director	le directeur artistique
artwork	l'illustration *f*
audience	le public
the ad has to reach a certain audience	*cette publicité doit atteindre un certain public*
banner	le titre à la une d'un journal
body copy	le corps de l'annonce
brief	le brief
broadsheet	le journal grand format
we're going to advertise in the broadsheet and tabloid press	*nous allons faire de la publicité dans les journaux de grand format et dans les tabloïdes*
brochure	la brochure
canvass	prospecter, démarcher
we have canvassed a lot of potential customers	*nous avons démarché beaucoup de clients potentiels*
caption	le sous-titre
catalogue/catalog	le catalogue
this product is not included in our current catalogue/catalog	*ce produit n'est pas répertorié dans notre catalogue habituel*
circular	la circulaire
endorse	soutenir
endorsement	le soutien
endorsement by a well-known actress will boost sales	*le soutien d'une actrice célèbre fera remonter les ventes*
flier	le prospectus
freesheet	le gratuit
issue	la parution
jingle	le jingle, le sonal
the ad has a very catchy jingle	*cette publicité a un jingle très accrocheur*

layout	la mise en page
magazine	le magazine
we'll reach our audience through magazines	*nous atteindrons notre public à travers les magazines*
media	les médias
mass media	les médias
media coverage	le public atteint
outdoor advertising	l'emplacement *m* publicitaire
we've designed some posters for outdoor advertising	*nous avons conçu des affiches pour des emplacements publicitaires*
pamphlet	la plaquette
periodical	le périodique
poster	l'affiche *f*
prospectus	le prospectus
the company issued a shareholder prospectus	*la société a publié un prospectus pour ses actionnaires*
publication	une publication
ratings	l'indice *m* d'écoute
weekly TV ratings	*les indices d'écoute hebdomadaires de la télévision, l'audimat m*
readership	le nombre de lecteurs
slogan	le slogan
spot	le spot
TV spot	*le spot publicitaire*
sticker	l'autocollant *m*
tabloid	le tabloïde, le quotidien populaire
viewer	le téléspectateur
voice-over	le commentaire

Pricing

bargain (v)	négocier
ceiling	la limite, le plafonnement
price ceiling	le plafonnement de prix
creaming	prendre la crème/le meilleur
cut-price/cut-rate	la compression de prix
cut-price deals have reduced margins	*comprimer les prix réduit les marges*

discount	la réduction
elastic	élastique
fix	déterminer
going rate	le taux actuel
we should charge the going rate	*nous devrions facturer au taux actuel*
gross margin	la marge brute
index/retail price	le répertoire de prix
inelastic	fixe
introductory offer	l'offre *f* promotionnelle
knock down/mask-down	réduire
margin	la marge
mark up (v)	majorer
the retailer has marked up the price by 50%	*le détaillant a majoré les prix de 50%*
MRP (Manufacturer's Recommended Price)	le prix public conseillé
overheads	les frais *m* généraux
premium	la prime
rate	le tarif
refund (n)/(v)	le remboursement/rembourser
retail price	le prix au détail
surcharge (n)/(v)	le prix excessif/surtaxer
value	la valeur

Public relations

identity	l'identité *f*
corporate identity	l'identité *f* de l'entreprise
image	l'image *f*
corporate image	l'image de l'entreprise
lobby (v)	influencer, intervenir
we are lobbying the Minister for/Secretary of Agriculture	*nous intervenons auprès du Ministre de l'Agriculture*
press officer	l'attaché *m* de presse
press relations	les relations *f* avec la presse
press release	un communiqué de presse
we have issued a press release	*nous avons publié un communiqué de presse*
sponsor (v)	parrainer, sponsoriser
sponsorship	le parrainage publicitaire

PERSONNEL

absent	absent(e)
absenteeism	l'absentéisme *m*
absenteeism has risen due to bad health	*l'absentéisme a augmenté en raison de problèmes de santé*
canteen	la cantine
career	la carrière
conditions	les conditions *f*
working conditions	les conditions de travail
conditions of employment	les conditions d'embauche
core time	les horaires *m* fixes
core time is between 10:00 and 15:00	*les horaires fixes sont entre 10 h et 15 h*
employ	employer
employee	l'employé(e)
employer	l'employeur (-euse)
equal opportunity	l'égalité *f* des chances
this company has an equal opportunities policy	*cette société a une politique d'égalité des chances*
human resources	les ressources *f* humaines
job centre/center	l'agence *f* nationale pour l'emploi (ANPE)
job sharing	le partage des fonctions
job satisfaction	la satisfaction dans le travail
leader	le dirigeant
leadership	la direction
we are looking for leadership qualities	*nous cherchons des qualités de dirigeant*
liaison	la relation
close liaison with the staff	*une relation privilégiée avec le personnel*
manpower	la main d'œuvre
manpower planning	la planification de la main d'œuvre
pool	le regroupement, le pool
secretaries are drawn from a pool	*les secrétaires sont recrutées dans un pool*
profession	la profession
punctuality	la ponctualité
shift	l'équipe *f*

EMPLOYMENT LAW, see page 122

the first shift is from 06:00 to 14:00	*la première équipe travaille de 6 h à 14 h*
night shift	l'équipe de nuit
shopfloor	l'atelier *m*, les ouvriers *m*
shop steward	le porte-parole des ouvriers
sick note	le certificat médical
trade union	le syndicat ouvrier
vacation	les vacances *f* /les congés *m*
working hours	les heures de travail
working hours are currently 37 per week	*actuellement, on travaille 37 heures par semaine*
work load	la charge de travail

Types of jobs

blue-collar worker	le col bleu
board of directors	le conseil d'administration
clerk	l'employé(e)
management	le cadre
junior/middle/senior	inférieur/moyen/supérieur
manager	le directeur
line/staff	le chef hiérarchique/le directeur du personnel
manual	manuel (-elle)
manual worker	le travailleur manuel
skilled	qualifié(e)
semi-skilled/unskilled	semi-qualifié(e)/non-qualifié(e)
shift workers	les équipes *f*
staff	le personnel *m*
superior	le supérieur
his superior reports to the Managing Director/CEO	*son supérieur fait un rapport au PDG*
white-collar workers	les employés de bureau

Disputes

grievance	la revendication
their grievances include low pay and long hours	*leurs revendications englobent les bas salaires et les heures de travail trop longues*
industrial action	la grève
industrial relations	les relations humaines dans l'entreprise

COMPANY POSITIONS, see page 28

industrial unrest	l'agitation f ouvrière
picket (n)/(v)	le piquet de grève/mettre un piquet de grève
the factory was picketed during the strike	*l'usine a été mise sous piquet de grève*
strike (n)/(v)	la grève/faire la grève
work to rule	la grève du zèle

Recruitment

applicant	le postulant
application form	le dossier de candidature
apply for a job	postuler
appoint	nommer
candidate	le candidat, la candidate
c.v. (curriculum vitae/resumé)	le C.V. (curriculum vitae)
fill a position	occuper un poste
hire	embaucher
interview, to come for	se présenter à un entretien
interviewee	la personne qui se présente à l'entretien
interviewer	la personne qui mène l'entretien
job description	la description du poste
qualifications	les qualifications f
qualified	qualifié(e)
we're only interested in qualified personnel	*nous sommes uniquement intéressés par un personnel qualifié*
well-qualified/unqualified	très qualifié(e)/non-qualifié(e)
recruitment	le recrutement
reference	la référence
they followed up her references	*ils ont pris en compte ses références*
select	choisir
vacancy	le poste vacant
I'm afraid we have no vacancies at present	*je regrette, mais nous n'avons pas de postes vacants pour l'instant*

Leaving

dismissal	le licenciement

fire (v) — **renvoyer, mettre à la porte**
he was fired for stealing — ***il a été mis à la porte pour vol***

hand in one's notice — **donner à quelqu'un son préavis**

lay-off (n)/(v) — **la mise au chômage/mettre au chômage**

redundant/laid off — **licencié(e)**
2,000 workers will be made redundant/laid off — ***2000 ouvriers vont être licenciés***

resign — **démissionner**

resignation — **la démission**

retire — **partir à la retraite**

retirement — **la retraite**
he was offered early retirement — ***on lui a proposé la pré-retraite***

Assessment

appraise/review — **évaluer**
all the staff are appraised/ reviewed annually — ***l'ensemble du personnel est évalué chaque année***

appraisal/review — **l'évaluation** *f*

competence — **la compétence**

grade — **le niveau**

perform — **effectuer**

performance appraisal — **l'évaluation** *f* **du résultat**

probation — **l'essai** *m*
he's on probation for 6 months — ***il a été engagé à l'essai pour 6 mois***

Training & development

apprentice — **le/la stagiaire, l'apprenti(e)**
the company takes on 5 apprentices a year — ***la société prend 5 stagiaires par an***

apprenticeship — **l'apprentissage** *m*

course — **le stage**

experience — **l'expérience** *f*

facilitate — **faciliter**
the training should facilitate decision-making — ***la formation devrait faciliter les prises de décision***

mentor — **le guide**

on-the-job training — **la formation sur le tas**

promote — **promouvoir**

progress — **progresser**

seminar	le séminaire
we are organizing a seminar on leadership skills	*nous organisons un séminaire sur les fonctions de dirigeant*
train (v)	former
training	la formation
workshop	l'atelier *m* de formation

Remuneration

collective bargaining	la négociation collective
benefit	l'avantage *m*
fringe benefit	l'avantage en nature
company cars are a common fringe benefit	*les voitures de société sont des avantages en nature courants*
sickness benefit	les prestations de l'assurance maladie
compensate	dédommager
deduction	la déduction
my take-home pay after all deductions is very little	*mon salaire net après déduction est très bas*
incentive	l'encouragement *m*
income	le revenu
overtime	les heures *f* supplémentaires
you can make up the wage with overtime	*vous pouvez augmenter votre salaire par des heures supplémentaires*
pay (n)/(v)	la paye/payer
pay package	l'enveloppe *f* des salaires
payroll	la fiche de paye, le bulletin de salaire
pension	la retraite
perk	avantages *m* accessoires
profit-sharing	l'intéressement *m*
the employees all benefit from a profit-sharing scheme	*les employés bénéficient d'un système d'intéressement*
raise (n)/(v)	l'augmentation *f* /augmenter
I just received a salary raise	*le viens de recevoir une augmentation de salaire*
salary	le salaire
share option	l'actionnariat *m*
wage	la paye

PRODUCTION

Quality

accurate	**précis(e)**
accuracy	**la précision**
assess	**estimer**
defect	**le défaut**
the defect was caused by a faulty machine	*le défaut a été provoqué par une machine défectueuse*
evaluate	**évaluer**
inspect	**inspecter**
ISO	**ISO**
quality assurance/control	**l'assurance** f **qualité**
quality circle	**le cercle de qualité**
the plant has set up quality circles	*l'usine f a développé des cercles de qualité*
reject (n)/(v)	**la mise au rebut/rejeter, mettre au rebut**
reject rate	**le taux de mise au rebut**
the reject rate has fallen as a result of quality control	*le taux de mise au rebut a chuté depuis la mise en place des contrôles qualité*
scrap (n)/(v)	**le déchet/mettre hors service**
zero defect	**zéro défaut**
we are aiming for zero defect production	*nous visons une production zéro défaut*

Process

assemble	**l'assemblage** m
assembly	**assembler**
assembly line	**la chaîne de montage**
the assembly line has been automated	*la chaîne de montage a été automatisée*
automate	**automatiser**
automation	**l'automatisation** f
component	**la pièce** f
continuous process	**le procédé ininterrompu**
convert	**convertir**
efficiency	**l'efficacité** f
efficient	**efficace**

finished goods	les produits *m* finis
goods	la marchandise
intermittent production	une production interrompue
line assembly	la production à la chaîne
line worker	le travailleur à la chaîne
off-the-shelf	immédiatement disponible
produce (n)	produire
production	la production

Planning

backlog	l'arriéré *m*
there is a backlog of orders to deal with	*il faut traiter les commandes en cours*
batch	le lot de marchandise
batch size	la taille des lots
capacity	la capacité
we are working at full capacity	*nous travaillons au maximum de nos capacités*
critical path analysis	l'analyse *f* du chemin critique
cycle time	la durée du cycle
delivery cycle	le cycle de livraison
downtime	le temps d'immobilisation
machine downtime costs money	*le temps d'immobilisation des machines coûte de l'argent*
flow rate	le flux
idle	à l'arrêt
we can't afford for the machines to be idle	*nous ne pouvons pas nous permettre de mettre les machines à l'arrêt*
job lot	le lot d'articles divers
lead time	le délai de livraison
the lead time is too long	*le délai de livraison est trop long*
make-to-order	la production selon commande
make-to-stock	la production selon stock
output	le rendement
productive	productif (-ive)
productivity	la productivité
productivity levels have increased	*les niveaux de productivité ont augmenté*

prototype	**le prototype**
schedule	**le programme**
set-up time	**le temps de montage**
slack	**stagnant(e)**
throughput	**le rendement**
work-in progress	**les travaux** *m* **en cours**

Resources & stock

bill of materials	**la nomenclature**
equip	**équiper**
equipment	**l'équipement** *m*
just-in-time	**juste dans les délais**
machine	**la machine**
machinery	**la machinerie**
MRP (Materials Requirements Planning)	**la planification des matériaux requis**
materials handling	**la gestion des fournitures**
raw materials	**les matières** *f* **premières**
stock (n)/(v)	**le stock/stocker**
stock levels	**les niveaux** *m* **de stock**
in stock	**en stock**
we have just one left in stock	*il nous en reste un seul en stock*
out of stock	**hors-stock, en rupture de stock**
stock control	**le contrôle des stocks**
store (n)/(v)	**les réserves/emmagasiner**
storage	**le stockage**

Maintenance

break down	**tomber en panne**
this machine has never broken down	*cette machine n'est jamais tombée en panne*
failure	**la panne**
fault	**le défaut**
faulty	**défectueux (-euse)**
maintain	**entretenir**
maintenance	**l'entretien** *m,* **la maintenance**
repair (n)/(v)	**la réparation/réparer**
reliable	**fiable**
reliability	**la fiabilité**
shut-down (n)/(v)	**la fermeture/fermer**

PURCHASING

auction (n)	**la vente aux enchères**
buy	**acheter**
buyer, junior/senior	**le responsable des achats/le directeur des achats**
purchaser	**l'acquéreur** *m*
source	**la source**
you should have at least two sources	*vous devriez avoir au moins deux sources*
spend (n)/(v)	**la dépense/dépenser**
total purchasing spend is over 1 million	*la dépense globale est de plus d'un million*
supply (v)	**fournir**
supplies	**les fournitures** *f*
supplier	**le fournisseur**
vendor	**le vendeur, la vendeuse**

Functions

inventory management	**la gestion des stocks**
inventory control	**le contrôle des stocks**
logistics	**la logistique**
materials management	**la gestion des matériaux**
vendor appraisal	**l'appréciation** *f* **du vendeur**
the criteria for vendor appraisal include price, quality and delivery	*les critères d'appréciation d'un vendeur englobent le prix, la qualité et la livraison*

Finance

bill	**la facture**
billing	**la facturation**
we prefer quarterly billing	*nous préférons une facturation trimestrielle*
currency	**la devise**
weak/strong currency	**une faible devise/une devise forte**
currency fluctuations	**les fluctuations des devises**

Supply & demand

buyers'/sellers' market	**le marché favorable au vendeur/à l'acheteur**

demand (n)	la demande
under-demand	la sous-demande
prices are low because of under-demand	*les prix sont bas à cause de la sous-demande*
over-demand	la sur-demande
supply	l'approvisionnement *m*
under-supply	le sous-approvisionnement
over-supply	le sur-approvisionnement

Tendering process

accept	accepter
our offer was accepted	*notre offre a été acceptée*
call for tenders	l'appel *m* d'offres
the call for tenders was published in the press	*l'appel d'offres a été publié dans la presse*
open/closed tender	une offre illimitée/limitée
reject	rejeter
submit a tender/an offer	soumettre un devis/une offre
tender specifications	le cahier des charges
the tender specifications are very detailed	*le cahier des charges est très détaillé*
tender evaluation	l'estimation *f* des coûts

Documents

letter of intent	la lettre d'intention
we sent the supplier a letter of intent	*nous avons fait parvenir au fournisseur une lettre d'intention*
purchase order	la commande

Price negotiation

bottom-line	le bénéfice net
our bottom-line was £150,000	*notre bénéfice net a représenté £ 150 000*
cut	la réduction
we forced a 10% price cut on all our suppliers	*nous avons imposé une réduction de 10 % à tous nos fournisseurs*
margin	la marge
target price	le prix de référence

COMPANY DEPARTMENTS

SALES

client	la clientèle
customer	le client, la cliente
end-user	le consommateur
give-away	le cadeau publicitaire
we usually supply give-aways such as pens	nous avons l'habitude de distribuer des cadeaux publicitaires tels que des stylos
prospect	le prospect, le client potentiel
sales call	la vente par téléphone, l'entretien m téléphonique de vente
I've got one more sales call to make	il me reste un entretien téléphonique de vente à faire
sales conference	la réunion commerciale
target	l'objectif m
we have a very ambitious sales target this year	cette année, nous avons un objectif commercial très ambitieux
sample	l'échantillon m

Selling people & organisation

field sales	la vente sur le terrain
we've got a team of 3 field salespeople	nous avons trois équipes de vente
sales area	la zone de vente
the country is divided into four sales areas	le pays est réparti en quatre zones de vente
sales assistant/manager	le délégué/directeur commercial
salesforce	la force de vente

Types of selling

door-to-door sales	la vente à domicile
direct sales	la vente directe
hard selling	la vente agressive
hard selling doesn't work in this business	la vente agressive ne marche pas dans ce domaine
personal selling	la vente personnelle
soft selling	la vente par suggestion
telephone sales	la vente par téléphone

Sales

Industries and Professions

CONSTRUCTION

Materials used in construction

asphalt	l'asphalte *m*
brick	la brique
red brick	la brique rouge
cement	le ciment
clay	l'argile *f*
concrete	le béton
pre-fabricated concrete	le béton pré-fabriqué
reinforced concrete	le béton armé
glass	le verre
frosted glass	le verre dépoli

plain glass	**le verre clair**
reinforced glass	**le verre armé**
safety glass	**le verre de sécurité**
gravel	**le gravier**
macadam	**le macadam**
masonry	**la maçonnerie**
mortar	**le mortier**
plastic	**le plastique**
slate	**l'ardoise** *f*
steel	**l'acier** *m*
steel girder	**la poutre métallique**
stone	**la pierre**
cobble stone	**le pavé**
tarmac	**le macadam goudronné**
tiles	**les tuiles** *f*
timber	**le bois de construction**
uPVC	**le PVC**
wood	**le bois**
wooden beam	**la poutre en bois**
wooden plank	**la planche en bois**

Planning regulations in this area prohibit the use of prefabricated concrete.

Les règlements d'organisation urbaine de ce quartier interdisent l'utilisation de béton pré-fabriqué.

Professions in construction

architect	**l'architecte** *m/f*
brick layer	**le maçon**
builder	**l'entrepreneur (-euse)**
carpenter	**le charpentier**
designer	**le concepteur (-trice)**
developer	**le promoteur (-trice)**
draughtsman	**le dessinateur (-trice)**
engineer	**l'ingénieur**
civil	**l'ingénieur civil**
sanitary	**le technicien en équipement sanitaire**
structural	**le constructeur (-trice)**
glazier	**le vitrier**
joiner	**le menuisier**
painter	**le peintre**
planner	**l'urbaniste** *f/m*

Construction

PROPERTY, see page 110

plasterer	**le plâtrier**
plumber	**le plombier**
surveyor	**le géomètre**
quantity surveyor	**le métreur (-euse)**

Our on-site management team consists of an architect, responsible for drawing up the plan, a civil engineer and a surveyor.

Notre équipe de terrain est composée d'un architecte, responsable de dessiner le plan, d'un ingénieur civil et d'un géomètre.

Processes in construction

to build	**bâtir**
to chart	**établir un graphique**
to construct	**construire**
to cool	**refroidir**
to demolish	**démolir**
to design	**concevoir**
to dig	**creuser**
to draft	**rédiger**
to draw	**dessiner**
to erect	**ériger**
to excavate	**creuser**
to heat	**chauffer**
to install	**installer**
to maintain	**entretenir**
to measure	**mesurer**
to plan	**planifier**
to refurbish	**restaurer**
to renovate	**rénover**
to repair	**réparer**
to replace	**remplacer**
to scaffold	**échafauder**
to sketch	**esquisser**
to ventilate	**ventiler**
to wire	**faire l'installation électrique**

Our company specialises in refurbishing old houses: everything from designing the plans to carrying out the job.

Notre entreprise est spécialisée dans la rénovation des maisons anciennes: nous nous occupons de tout, de la conception des plans jusqu'à l'exécution des travaux.

INDUSTRIES AND PROFESSIONS

ENGINEERING

Branches of engineering

architectural engineering	l'architecture f
chemical engineering	la chimie
civil engineering	le génie civil
drainage engineering	la technique f d'assainissement
electrical engineering	l'électrotechnique f
electronic engineering	l'électronique f
fire protection engineering	la technique de protection contre le feu
highway engineering	les Ponts et Chaussées
hydraulic engineering	la technique hydraulique
industrial engineering	l'organisation industrielle
marine engineering	le génie maritime
mechanical engineering	la mécanique
mining and metallurgical engineering	la technique minière et métallurgique
nuclear engineering	la technique nucléaire
petroleum production engineering	les techniques de production pétrolière
production engineering	les techniques de la production
railway engineering	le génie ferroviaire
safety engineering	la technique sécuritaire
sanitary engineering	la technique d'équipement sanitaire
structural engineering	la construction
welding engineering	la technique de soudure

We plan to call in a safety engineering company to advise us on improving standards.

Nous avons l'intention de faire appel à une entreprise de technique sécuritaire pour nous conseiller quant à l'amélioration des conditions à l'intérieur de l'entreprise.

Applications of engineering

boiler	la chaudière
boring	le forage
bridge	le pont
dye	la teinture
electricity supply	l'alimentation f en électricité

Engineering

gas manufacture	**la production de gaz**
hydraulics	**l'hydraulique** *f*
mining	**l'exploitation minière**
paper manufacture	**la fabrique de papier**
power generation	**la production d'énergie**
power transmission	**la transmission d'énergie**
printing	**l'imprimerie** *f*
shipbuilding	**la construction navale**

Equipment in engineering

boiler	**la chaudière**
crane	**la grue**
gas engine	**le moteur à gaz**
machine tools	**les machines-outils** *f*
pump	**la pompe**
turbine/engine	**la turbine**
steam	**la turbine à vapeur**
water	**la turbine hydraulique**

This boiler has an auxiliary safety valve to prevent a build-up of pressure.

Cette chaudière possède une valve de sécurité complémentaire pour empêcher une augmentation de pression.

Processes in treating metals

to anneal	**recuire**
to anodize	**poser une anode**
to electroplate	**plaquer**
to forge	**forger**
to found	**fondre**
to galvanize	**galvaniser**
to grind	**concasser**
to harden	**durcir**
to mint	**monnayer**
to plate	**blinder**
to roll	**laminer**
to temper	**tremper**
to terneplate	**étamer**
to tinplate	**blinder au fer blanc**

Some of our customers ask us to galvanize the metal in order to strengthen it.

Certains de nos clients nous ont demandé de galvaniser le métal afin de le renforcer.

FOOD AND CATERING

The meals

breakfast	**le petit-déjeuner**
lunch	**le déjeuner**
dinner	**le dîner**
picnic	**le pique-nique**
snack	**la collation**

The elements of food

carbohydrates	**les hydrates** *m* **de carbone**
fats	**les matières** *f* **grasses**
proteins	**les protéines** *f*
vitamins	**les vitamines** *f*
minerals	**les minéraux** *m*

Types of food

cereals	**les céréales** *f*
dairy products	**les produits** *m* **laitiers**
drinks	**les boissons** *f*
eggs	**les œufs** *m*
fats	**les matières** *f* **grasses**
fish	**le poisson**
fruit	**les fruit** *m*
game	**le gibier**
herbs	**les fines herbes** *f*
meat	**la viande**
nuts	**les noix**
organic food	**les aliments** *m* **biologiques**
poultry	**les volailles** *f*
preserves	**les conservateurs**
pulses/lentils	**les plantes** *f* **légumineuses**
sauce	**la sauce**
seafood	**les fruits** *m* **de mer**
sweets	**les sucreries** *f*
vegetables	**les légumes** *m*

We have changed the ingredients in many of our products, because of the danger to health caused by fats and sweets.

Nous avons changé les ingrédients de beaucoup de nos produits à cause du risque pour la santé provoqué par les matières grasses et les sucres.

DINING OUT, see page 27

Parts of a meal

aperitif	**l'apéritif** *m*
starter/first course	**l'entrée** *f*
soup	**la soupe**
salad	**la salade**
main course	**le plat principal**
dessert	**le dessert**
cheese and biscuits	**le fromage et les biscuits** *m*

Growing processes in food-making

to fatten	**engraisser**
to fertilize	**fertiliser**
to germinate	**faire germer**
to grow	**pousser**
to harvest	**moissonner, récolter**
to hatch	**éclore**
to milk	**traire**
to pick	**piocher**
to plough/plow	**labourer**
to propagate	**propager**
to rear	**élever, cultiver**
to slaughter	**abattre**
to sow	**semer**

We guarantee that the animals have been organically reared and slaughtered in a humane way.

Nous garantissons que les animaux ont été élevés biologiquement et qu'ils ont été abattus de façon humaine.

Food preparation

to bake	**cuire**
to boil	**bouillir**
to chop up	**hacher**
to cook	**cuire, cuisiner**
to cure	**saurer**
to cut	**couper**
into pieces/slices	**en morceaux** *m*/**en tranches** *f*
to cut up	**découper**
to fry	**frire**
to grill	**griller**
to heat	**chauffer**

to marinate	**mariner**
to melt	**faire fondre**
to pickle	**saumurer**
to roast	**rôtir**
to salt	**saler**
to smoke	**fumer**
to stew	**laisser mijoter**
to sweeten	**sucrer**
to toast	**griller**

We cut up the fruit into small pieces before we put it into cans.

Nous découpons le fruit en petits morceaux avant de le mettre en conserve.

The business of catering

banquet hall	**la salle de banquet**
bar	**le bar**
buffet	**le buffet**
café	**le café-restaurant**
cafeteria	**la cafétéria**
chef	**le chef de cuisine**
coffeeshop	**le café**
cook	**le cuisinier**
diner *(person)*	**le dîneur (-euse)**
diner *(roadside)*	**le routier**
fast food	**la restauration rapide**
feast	**le festin**
meal	**le repas**
pub	**le bistrot**
refreshment	**le rafraîchissement**
restaurateur	**le restaurateur**
serve	**servir**
snack	**la collation**
teahouse	**le salon de thé**
waiter	**le serveur**
drinks waiter	**le sommelier**
waitress	**la serveuse**

The conference centre/center provides three main function rooms and is able to serve buffet meals for up to 300 delegates.

Le centre de conférences offre trois principales salles de réunions et peut servir un buffet pour 300 délégués.

INFORMATION TECHNOLOGY

Source of information

archive	**les archives** f
databank	**la banque de données**
database	**la base de données**
file	**le fichier**
library	**la bibliothèque**

The customer database contains the names and addresses of all our customers.   ***La base de données de la clientèle contient les noms et adresses de tous nos clients.***

The representation of information

digital data	**les données** f **numériques**
digitize	**numériser**
encipher	**chiffrer**
image	**l'image** f
message	**le message**
signal	**le signal**
electric signal	**le signal électrique**
electromagnetic signal	**le signal électromagnétique**
transformation	**la transformation**

If you digitize data, you can store it in a digital form, i.e. as a series of 1s and 0s.   ***Si vous numérisez les données, vous pouvez les stocker sous forme numérique, par ex. en une série de 1 et 0.***

The storage of information

bit	**l'unité** f **binaire**
byte	**l'octet** m
CD-ROM	**le disque optique numérique (DON), le CD-ROM**
data	**les données** f
data recording	**l'enregistrement** m **de données**
magnetic data recording	**l'enregistrement magnétique de données**
optical data recording	**l'enregistrement optique de données**
disk	**le disque**

INDUSTRIES AND PROFESSIONS

floppy disk	la disquette
hard disk	le disque dur
compact disk	le disque compact
memory	la mémoire
random access memory	la mémoire à accès direct
read-only memory (ROM)	la mémoire morte (ROM)

The transmission and processing of information

amplifier	l'amplificateur m
computer	l'ordinateur m
computer system	le système informatique
computer network	le réseau informatique
electrical impulses	les impulsions f électriques
microphone	le microphone
radio communication systems	le système de radio communications
radio transmitter	le transmetteur radio, l'émetteur m radio
signal	le signal
electronic signal	le signal électronique
electromagnetic signal	le signal électromagnétique
telephone	le téléphone
telephone network	le réseau téléphonique
teletype networks	le réseau télétypique
television	la télévision

The new Pentium® chip is at the heart of the system, processing huge amounts of data at incredible speeds.

La nouvelle puce Pentium® est au coeur du système, elle traite un grand nombre de données à des vitesses incroyables.

Processes

to convert	convertir
to degrade	dégrader
to distort	distordre
to receive	recevoir
to transmit	transmettre

This equipment can convert the old analog signals into digital signals.

Cet équipement peut convertir les anciens signaux analogiques en signaux numériques.

IT

TELECOMMUNICATIONS, see page 112

PHARMACEUTICALS AND CHEMICALS

Chemicals and life

alkaloids	**les alcaloïdes** m
carbohydrates	**les hydrates** m **de carbone**
cholesterol	**le cholestérol**
coloration	**la coloration**
drugs	**les produits pharmaceutiques, les drogues** f
enzymes	**les enzymes** f
hormones	**les hormones** f
lipids	**les lipides** m
nucleic acids	**les acides** m **nucléiques**
Deoxyribonucleic acid (DNA)	**l'acide désoxyribonucléique (ADN)**
Ribonucleic acid (RNA)	**l'acide ribonucléique (ARN)**
peptides	**les peptides** m
pigments	**les pigments** m
chlorophyll	**la chlorophylle**
melanin	**la mélanine**
proteins	**les protéines** f
amino acid	**les acides aminés**
glutamine	**l'acide glutamique**
gluten	**le gluten**
keratin	**la kératine**
myoglobin	**la myoglobine**
steroids	**les stéroïdes** m
vitamins	**les vitamines** f

As the lack of any hormone may cause a major deficiency, we now synthesize most of them artificially.

Comme une carence hormonale peut provoquer une déficience importante, nous synthétisons la plupart des hormones de façon artificielle.

Body systems

autonomic nervous system	**le système nerveux autonome**
cardiovascular system	**le système cardio-vasculaire**
central nervous system	**le système nerveux central**
digestive system	**le système digestif**
excretory system	**le système d'élimination**

INDUSTRIES AND PROFESSIONS

Pharmaceuticals and Chemicals

histamine response system	**le système de réponse histaminique**
immune response system	**le système immunitaire**
reproductive system	**le système reproductif**
skeletal muscle system	**le système musculaire**

Our new digestive tablets help with the ingestion, digestion and absorption of food.

Nos nouvelles pilules digestives facilitent l'ingestion, la digestion ainsi que l'absorption des aliments.

Drugs

atropins	**les atropines** f
analgesics	**les analgésiques** m
salicylic acid	**l'acide** m **salicylique**
anaesthetics	**les anesthésiques** m
chloroform	**le chloroforme**
cocaine	**la cocaïne**
procaine	**la procaïne**
antibiotics	**les antibiotiques** m
penicillin	**la pénicilline**
streptomycin	**la streptomycine**
antiseptics	**les antiseptiques** m
beta blockers	**les béta-blocants** m
chemotherapeutics	**les produits** m **chimiothérapeutiques**
quinine	**la quinine**
sulfa drug	**les produits sulfatés**
hallucinogens	**les hallucinogènes** m
cannabis	**le cannabis**
hashish	**le hachisch**
marijuana	**la marijuana**
mescaline	**la mescaline**
narcotics	**les stupéfiants** m
heroin	**l'héroïne** f
methadone	**la méthadone**
morphine	**la morphine**
opium	**l'opium** m
sedatives	**les sédatifs** m
barbiturates	**les barbituriques** m
thalidomide	**la thalidomide**
stimulants	**les stimulants** m
amphetamine	**les amphétamines** f

caffeine	la caféine
tranquillizers	les tranquillisants *m*
diazepam	le diazépam
others	autres
antacids	les antacides *m*
antihistamine	l'antihistamine *f*
diuretic	les diurétiques
ephedrine	l'éphédrine *f*
laxative	les laxatifs *m*

Some anaesthetics are used before or during surgery to depress the central nervous system.

Certains anesthésiques sont utilisés avant ou pendant une opération afin de diminuer le fonctionnement du système nerveux.

The drug business

ethical drugs	les médicaments *m* sur ordonnance
generic drugs	les médicaments génériques
me-too products	les produits copiés
prescription drugs	les médicaments sur ordonnance
proprietary drugs	les médicaments en vente libre
patent drugs	les médicaments brevetés
veterinary pharmaceuticals	les produits *m* vétérinaires

Proprietary drugs are sold over the counter; ethical drugs may be obtained legally only with a prescription from an authorized health-care provider.

Les médicaments sans ordonnance sont en vente libre; les autres médicaments ne peuvent être obtenus légalement qu'à partir d'une ordonnance d'un médecin.

Branches of medicine

clinical medicine	la médecine clinique
preventive medicine	la médecine préventive
fringe medicine	la médecine alternative
alternative medicine	la médecine parallèle
complementary medicine	la médecine complémentaire
holistic medicine	la médecine holistique
unorthodox medicine	la médecine douteuse
folk medicine	la médecine populaire

PROPERTY

The types of property

apartment/flat	**un appartement**
furnished apartment	**un appartement meublé**
studio apartment	**le studio**
apartment block/block of flats	**le pâté de maisons**
bungalow	**le bungalow**
chalet	**le chalet**
chateau	**le château**
consulate	**le consulat**
duplex/two-storey house	**une maison en duplex**
embassy	**une ambassade**
estate	**le domaine**
farmhouse	**la ferme**
field	**le champs**
grounds	**les terrains** *m*
hall	**l'entrée** *f*
house	**la maison**
country house	**la maison de campagne**
ranch house	**le ranch**
tenement house	**un immeuble d'habitation**
terraced (row) house	**une maison de rangée**
town house	**une maison urbaine**
lodge	**le pavillon**
mansion	**l'hôtel particulier,**
	le manoir
office	**le bureau**
official residence	**la résidence officielle**
palace	**le palais**
park	**le parc**
penthouse	**un appartement sous les toits**
plot	**le lot**
property	**la propriété**
stately home	**le château**
villa	**la villa**

Our client requires 350 square metres of office space, fully equipped with telecommunications connections, and in a central location.

Notre client demande 350m² de surface-bureau, entièrement équipé en télécommunications, dans le centre ville.

The relationship with property

boarder	le pensionnaire
homeowner	le propriétaire
leaseholder	le loueur à bail
lessee	le locataire à bail
lessor	le bailleur
lodger	le locataire
occupier	l'occupant(e)
owner	le propriétaire
resident	le résident
paying guest	le pensionnaire
renter	le loueur
squatter	le squatter
tenant	le bailleur

Under the terms of this lease the landlord, Mr Brown, grants possession and use of the property at this address to you as tenant or lessee for a term of 25 years.

Dans les conditions de ce bail, le propriétaire, M. Brown, vous accorde la possession et l'usage de la propriété de cette adresse, en tant que locataire pour une durée de 25 ans.

The legal aspects of property

assign	attribuer
convey	céder un bien
conveyance	la cession d'un bien
freehold	propriété foncière perpétuelle
lease/let (v)	louer à bail
leasehold	le bail
hereditament	biens transmissibles par héritage
let/lease/rental (n)	la location
let/lease/ (out) (v)	louer à bail
sublet (v)	sous-louer
sublet (n)	la sous-location
ownership	la propriété
rent (n)	le loyer
tenure	la jouissance
trust, in	à charge

As a potential buyer of the freehold, it is important to check the seller's title to the property.

En tant qu'acheteur potentiel de la propriété, il est important de vérifier le titre du vendeur à la propriété.

TELECOMMUNICATIONS

Systems in telecommunications

cable	le câble
cablegram	le câblogramme
electronic mail	le courrier électronique
facsimile/fax	le télécopieur, le fax
teleconferencing	la téléconférence
telegram	le télégramme
telegraphy	la télégraphie
telephony	la téléphonie
videoconferencing	la vidéoconférence
wire	le fil (électrique)
wireless telegraphy	la télégraphie sans fil

Our new videoconferencing equipment allows two or more people at different locations to communicate written, spoken and visual information to each other.

Notre nouvelle installation de vidéoconférence permet la communication d'informations écrites, orales et visuelles entre deux personnes ou plus situées à des endroits différents.

Technology in telecommunications

asynchronous transfer mode	le mode de transfert asynchrone
bandwidth	la largeur de bande
converter	le convertisseur
data	les données *f*
analog data	les données analogiques
digital data	les données numériques
transfer (v) data	transmettre les données
modem	le modem
fax modem	le fax modem
multiplexing	le multiplexage
time-division multiplexing	le multiplexage par répartition dans le temps (MRT)
network	le réseau
Internet	l'Internet *m*
local area net (LAN)	le réseau local
wide-area networks	les réseaux longue distance
signal	le signal
switching	la commutation
packet switching	la commutation de paquets

The A44 modem enables computer data to be transmitted over a telephone line at very high speeds.

Le modem A44 permet la transmission par ligne téléphonique de données nformatiques à de trèsgrandes vitesses.

Equipment and devices in telecommunications

amplifier	**l'amplificateur** *m*
antenna	**l'antenne** *f*
cable	**le câble**
coaxial cables	**des câbles coaxiaux**
fibre/fiber optic cables	**des câbles de fibre optique**
circuit	**le circuit**
integrated circuit	**le circuit intégré**
printed circuit	**le circuit imprimé**
communications satellite	**les satellites de communication**
electric	**électrique**
electric circuit	**le circuit électrique**
electric switch	**le commutateur électrique**
headphone	**les écouteurs** *m*
headset	**le casque**
laser	**le laser**
loudspeaker	**le haut-parleur**
microphone	**le microphone**
microprocessor	**le microprocesseur**
microwave	**la micro-onde**
photoelectric cell	**la cellule photo-électrique**
radar	**le radar**
receiver	**le récepteur**
semiconductor	**le semi-conducteur**
switchboard	**le tableau de distribution**
telephone	**le téléphone**
car telephone	**le téléphone de voiture**
cellular telephone	**le téléphone cellulaire**
radio telephone	**le radio-téléphone**
telephone exchange	**la circonscription, le central téléphonique**
	le visiophon, le vidéophone
videophone	
transistor	**le transistor**
transmitter	**le transmetteur**

Standard coaxial cable can carry up to 132,000 messages simultaneously.

Le câble coaxial standard peut véhiculer jusqu'à 132 000 messages en même temps.

TEXTILES AND CLOTHING

Types of textiles

canvas	le canevas, la toile
cashmere	le cashemire
chintz	le chintz
corduroy	le velours côtelé
cotton	le coton
damask	le damas
denim	le dénim
flannel	la flanelle
gauze	la gaze
hessian	la toile de jute
jute	la jute
linen	le lin
mohair	le mohair
net	le filet, le tulle
satin	le satin
silk	la soie
synthetics	le synthétique
polymer	le polymère
rayon	la rayonne
vinyl fibre/fiber	la fibre vinyle
velvet	le velours
wool	la laine

Synthetics such as nylon and polyester, which are stronger than silk and lower in price, have led to a tremendous reduction in silk production and consumption.

Les synthétiques tels que le nylon et le polyester, qui sont plus résistants que la soie et moins chers, ont fait chuter la production et la consommation de la soie.

Processes in textile manufacture

to crochet	crocheter
to darn	repriser
to dye	teindre
to felt	feutrer
to knit	tricoter
to press	calandrer
to spin	filer
to twill	croiser
to weave	tisser

BANKING

The business of banking

retail banking	**la banque de détail**
wholesale or corporate banking	**la banque de gros**
universal or full-service banking	**la banque universelle**
investment banking	**la banque d'investissement**
merchant banking	**la banque d'affaires**
trustee banking	**la banque trustee**

We specialise in wholesale banking for corporate and institutional investors.

Nous sommes spécialisés dans les opérations bancaires de gros destinés à des investisseurs sociétaires et institutionnels.

The services provided

account	**le compte**
bank account	**le compte bancaire**
current/checking account	**le compte courant**
deposit account	**le compte de dépôt/à terme**
savings account	**le compte d'épargne**
time deposit account	**le compte à terme**
correspondent banking	**les opérations bancaires de correspondance**
credit	**le crédit**
credit card	**la carte de crédit**
credit limit	**la limite de crédit**
credit line	**la limite de découvert**
deposit	**le dépôt**
deposit account	**le compte à terme**
deposit box	**le coffre de dépôt**
foreign exchange	**les devises** *f* **étrangères**
interest	**l'intérêt** *m*
interest rate	**le taux d'intérêt**
fixed interest rate	**le taux d'intérêt fixe**
variable interest rate	**le taux d'intérêt variable**
investment	**l'investissement** *m*
investment counselling	**le conseil en investissement**
investment services	**les services** *m* **en investissement**
loan	**l'emprunt** *m*
short-term loan	**l'emprunt à court terme**
long-term loan	**l'emprunt à long terme**

FINANCE DEPARTMENT, see page 73

lend	prêter
letter of credit	la lettre de crédit
mortgage	l'hypothèque m
overdraft	le découvert
portfolio management	la gestion de portefeuille
project financing	le financement de projets
risk analysis	l'analyse f de risque
safe-deposit box	déposer dans un coffre
save	épargner
savings	les épargnes
savings account	le compte d'épargne
transfer	le transfert
bank transfer	le transfert bancaire
travellers' cheques/checks	les chèques de voyage

Our savings accounts offer very attractive rates of interest.

Nos comptes d'épargne offrent des taux d'intérêts très avantageux.

The profession of banking

bank manager	le directeur de banque
cashier	le caissier
customer advisor	le conseiller clientèle
dealer	le boursier
financial analyst	l'analyste m/f financier (-ière)
financier	le financier
investment advisor/counsellor	le conseiller d'investissement
investor	l'investisseur m
market maker	le contrepartiste
portfolio manager	le responsable portefeuille
security guard	le responsable de la sécurité
teller	le guichetier
trader	l'opérateur m

If you have money to invest, our investment advisors will be happy to discuss your needs.

Si vous avez de l'argent à investir, nos conseillers se feront un plaisir de discuter de vos besoins.

A portfolio manager can make day-to-day decisions about your investments.

Un responsable portefeuille peut prendre des décisions concernant vos investissements au jour le jour.

INSURANCE

Types of insurance

aviation insurance	l'assurance *f* de l'aviation
fire insurance	l'assurance incendie
credit insurance	l'assurance de crédit
group insurance	l'assurance collective
group life insurance	l'assurance vie collective
group health insurance	l'assurance maladie collective
group annuities	les rentes *f* collectives
health insurance	l'assurance maladie
permanent health insurance	l'assurance maladie permanente
liability insurance	l'assurance de responsabilité civile
life insurance/assurance	l'assurance-vie
marine insurance	l'assurance marine
motor/car insurance	l'assurance véhicule
comprehensive	l'assurance tous risques
third party, fire and theft	l'assurance tiers, incendie *m* et vol *m*
re-insurance	la réassurance
theft insurance	l'assurance vol
title insurance	l'assurance titre

Under the terms of your motor insurance, you are not covered for damage caused to your own car.

Dans les conditions de votre assurance véhicule, vous n'êtes pas couvert en cas de dégâts causés à votre propre voiture.

Your health insurance will pay you a regular sum if you are unable to work for more than 2 months.

Notre assurance maladie vous paiera des primes régulières si vous êtes dans l'incapacité de travailler pendant plus de 2 mois.

The elements of insurance

accidental occurrence	l'accident *m*
agreement	l'accord *m*
claim	la déclaration
reimburse	rembourser
commission	la commission
pay commission	payer une commission

contract	le contrat
hazard	le risque
loss	la perte
mutuality	la mutuelle
peril	le péril
insurable peril	le péril assurable
uninsurable peril	le péril non assurable
policy	la police (d'assurance)
cancel a policy	annuler une police
issue a policy	délivrer une police
policy coverage	la couverture d'une police
premium	la prime
annual premium	la prime annuelle
monthly premium	la prime mensuelle
pay a premium	payer une prime
regular premium	une prime régulière
single premium	la prime unique
rating	l'indice *m*
risk	le risque
insurable risk	le risque assurable
underwriting	la garantie
underwriting rates	l'indice d'assurance

If you want to make a claim, you must complete the form giving precise details of how the accident happened.

Si vous voulez faire une déclaration, vous devez remplir le formulaire en donnant des détails précis sur l'accident.

You can pay for your insurance by 1 annual premium or spread it over 12 monthly premiums.

Vous pouvez payer votre assurance en une prime annuelle ou répartie en 12 primes mensuelles.

Risks

accident	l'accident *m*
accidental damage	les dégâts *m* matériels
accidental loss	les pertes *f* accidentelles
breakdown	la panne
business interruption	l'arrêt *m* de travail
death	le décès
explosion	l'explosion *f*
fire	l'incendie *m*

| flood | l'inondation f |
| illness | la maladie |

If you insure yourself against business interruption, then we will pay out in the event that you are prevented for carrying out your normal business activities.

Si vous êtes assuré contre l'arrêt de travail, nous vous couvrirons au cas où vous seriez empêché de poursuivre vos activités professionnelles.

The people involved in insurance

actuary	l'actuaire m
adjuster	le dispatcheur
agent	l'agent m
broker	le courtier
insurer/underwriter	l'assureur m
insured	assuré(e)
policy holder	l'assuré(e)

Our actuaries apply the theories of probability and statistics and the principles of finance to problems of insurance.

Nos actuaires appliquent les lois de la probabilité et des statistiques, ainsi que les principes de la finance aux problèmes d'assurance.

Claims

cash	les espèces f
cash value	la valeur numéraire
claim damages	déclarer un sinistre
compensation	le dédommagement
damages	les dégâts
depreciation	la dépréciation
make a claim for damage	faire une déclaration de sinistre
make a claim for loss	faire une déclaration de perte
new for old	la valeur neuve pour de l'ancien
wear and tear	l'usure f

If you make a claim for damage or loss, then your compensation will be either on the basis of new for old or with a deduction for normal wear and tear.

Si vous faites une déclaration de sinistre ou de perte, votre dédommagement se fera soit sur la base du neuf pour de l'ancien, soit en tenant compte d'une déduction selon l'usure.

LAW

INDUSTRIES AND PROFESSIONS

General elements of law

action	le procès
bring an action against someone	intenter un procès à quelqu'un
award	la sentence arbitrale
capacity	la capacité
case	l'action *f*
civil case	l'action civile
criminal case	l'affaire pénale
claim	la réclamation
make a claim against someone	entreprendre une réclamation contre quelqu'un
compensation	le dédommagement
court	le tribunal
take someone to court	amener quelqu'un devant le tribunal
damage	le préjudice
damages	les dommages et intérêts
defendant	le défendeur, la défenderesse
dispute	le litige
settle a dispute	régler un litige
duty	le devoir
duty of care	le devoir de responsabilité
to impose a duty	imposer un devoir
fine	l'amende *f*
gross	flagrant(e)
gross incompetence	l'incompétence *f* flagrante
gross misconduct	le flagrant délit
gross negligence	la négligence flagrante
grounds	les causes *f*
judge	le juge
law	la loi
lawyer	l'avocat(e)
liability	la responsabilité
legislation	la législation
offence	le délit
offend	commettre un délit
offender	le délinquant
party	la partie
guilty party	la partie coupable

Law

LEGAL DEPARTMENT, see page 78

responsible party	la partie responsable
plaintiff	le demandeur, la partie demanderesse
prison	la prison
imprisonment	l'emprisonnement *m*
proceedings	les procédures *f*
prosecute	poursuivre
remedy	remédier
sentence	le jugement
sue	intenter un procès
terms	les sessions *f*
title	le titre
valid	valide
invalid	invalide
validity	la validité

Contract law

accept	accepter
acceptance	l'acceptation *f*
agreement	l'accord *m*
conditions of an agreement	les conditions *f* d'un accord
terms of an agreement	les termes *m* d'un accord
bid	l'appel *m*
breach	la violation
breach of contract	la violation d'un contrat
clause	la clause
compensation	le dédommagement
consideration	la considération
contract	le contrat
break a contract	rompre un contrat
enter into a contract	entrer en contrat
make a contract	faire un contrat
oral contract	un contrat oral
rescind a contract	résilier un contrat
terminate a contract	mettre fin à un contrat
written contract	un contrat écrit
intention to create legal relations	l'intention *f* de créer des relations légales
offer	l'offre *f*
make an offer	faire une offre
withdraw an offer	rejeter une offre
party	la partie
sue	poursuivre

INDUSTRIES AND PROFESSIONS

Law

Employment law

discriminate	discriminer
discriminate against someone on the basis of sex, race or religion	discriminer quelqu'un à cause de/en vertu du sexe, de la race ou de la religion
dismiss	licencier
dismissal	le licenciement
fire (v)	virer
lump sum	le paiement forfaitaire
misconduct	la faute
pension	la retraite
pensionable age	l'âge m de la retraite
pension off	mettre à la retraite
re-engage	réengager
re-engagement	le réengagement
redundant/laid off	licencié(e)
make someone redundant/lay someone off	licencier quelqu'un
redundancy/dismissal payment	le licenciement
reinstate	réintégrer
reinstatement	la réintégration
retire	partir à la retraite
retirement	la retraite
sack (v)	mettre à la porte
strike	faire grève
trade union	le syndicat

If you are in breach of the terms of your contract of employment, you can be dismissed. / *Si vous violez les conditions de votre contrat de travail, vous pouvez être licencié.*

Civil law

arbitrate	arbitrer
arbitration	l'arbitrage m
conveyancing	la procédure translative de propriété
damages	les dommages m et intérêts m
claim damages	réclamer des dommages et intérêts
liable	responsable
litigate	plaider
litigation	le litige
statute	la loi, l'ordonnance f

PERSONNEL DEPARTMENT, see page 86

TOURISM AND LEISURE

Outdoor leisure activities

archery	le tir à l'arc
bobsleighing/bobsledding	le bobsleigh
camping	le camping
caving	la spéléologie
curling	le curling
cycling	le cyclisme
diving	la plongée
deep-sea diving	la plongée sous-marine
skin diving	la plongée sous-marine autonome
exploring	l'expédition f
flying	l'aviation f
gliding	le vol à voile
hang gliding	le deltaplane
paragliding	le parapente
hiking	la randonnée
hunting	la chasse
jogging	la course
luging	la randonnée de traîneaux
mountaineering	la randonnée en montagne
orienteering	l'orientation f
riding	l'équitation f
rock-climbing	l'escalade f
shooting	le tir
skating	le patinage
ice hockey	le hockey sur glace
ice skating	le patinage sur glace
skiing	le ski
downhill skiing	le ski de piste
cross-country skiing	le ski de fond
langlauf	le ski de fond
ski-jumping	le saut en ski
water skiing	le ski nautique
snorkling	la plongée en tuba
surfing	le surf
wind-surfing	le windsurf
swimming	la nage
tobogganing	le toboggan

walking	la promenade
weight-training/lifting	l'haltérophilie f

Many people now take two holidays/vacations a year: a skiing holiday/vacation in winter and a beach holiday/vacation in summer.

Beaucoup de personnes partent à présent deux fois par an en vacances: des vacances de ski en hiver et des vacances à la mer en été.

Travel and Tourism

biking	le cyclisme
bus tour	le voyage en bus
business trip	le voyage d'affaires
cruise	la croisière
cycling	le cyclisme
driving	la conduite
excursion	l'excursion f
expedition	l'expédition f
grand tour	le grand voyage
hiking	la randonnée
journey/trip	le voyage
joy ride	le voyage de plaisance
motoring	l'automobilisme m
outing	le concours
package tour	le voyage organisé
pleasure trip	le voyage d'agrément
ramble	la randonnée pédestre
ride	la promenade
riding	l'équitation f
safari	le safari
shopping trip	la tournée d'achats
study holiday/vacation	les cours m de vacances
tour	le voyage
package tour	le voyage organisé
trek	le trekking
visit	la visite
voyage	le voyage
walking	la marche

Meditours are offering an autumn/fall cruise around the Mediterranean.

Meditours propose une croisière d'automne en Méditerranée.

English–French Business Dictionary

f	**feminine**
m	**masculine**
pl	**plural**
(adj)	**adjective**
(n)	**noun**
(v)	**verb**
qch.	**quelque chose**
qqn	**quelqu'un**
so.	**someone**
sth.	**something**

A

abandon an action renoncer aux poursuites/à un procès
abroad à l'étranger
absent absent(e)
absolute monopoly monopole absolu
accelerated depreciation amortissement accéléré
accept (v) *(agree, take sth.)* accepter
accept delivery of a shipment réceptionner des marchandises, prendre livraison d'un envoi
accept liability for sth. accepter la responsabilité de qch.
acceptable acceptable
acceptance acceptation *f*
account compte *m*
account executive responsable *m* de clientèle/de gestion de budget
account for rendre compte de
account in credit compte *m* créditeur
account on hold compte *m* bloqué
account, on en acompte
accountancy/accounting comptabilité *f*
accounts department service *m* de la comptabilité
accounts payable comptes *mpl* fournisseurs, dettes *fpl*
accounts receivable comptes clients *mpl*, créances *fpl*
accrue courir, s'accumuler
acknowledge receipt of a letter accuser réception d'une lettre

acquisition acquisition *f*
across-the-board général(e)
act of God catastrophe *f* naturelle
acting manager directeur (-trice) intérimaire
action for damages poursuite *f* en dommages-intérêts
actuals chiffres réels
ad valorem ad valorem, proportionnel
add on 10% for service ajouter 10% pour le service
additional charges frais *mpl* supplémentaires, supplément *m*
additional premium prime additionnelle
address (n) adresse *f*
address a letter adresser une lettre
address list répertoire *m*/fichier *m* d'adresses
adjourn a meeting lever la séance; ajourner une réunion
adjudication tribunal conseil *m* de prud'hommes; conseil *m* d'arbitrage
adjustment ajustement *m*, modification *f*
administration administration *f*, gestion *f*
administrative expenses frais administratifs, frais de gestion
admission charge/fee entrée *f*
advance (n) *(loan)* avance *f*
advance (v) *(lend)* avancer (de l'argent), prêter (de l'argent)
advance booking réservation *f* à l'avance
advance on account avance *f*, acompte *m*, provision *f*
advance payment paiement anticipé
advertise a new product faire de la publicité pour un produit nouveau
advertise a vacancy annoncer un poste
advertisement annonce *f*, publicité *f*
advertiser annonceur *m*
advertising agency agence *f* de publicité
advertising budget budget *m* de publicité
advertising rates tarifs *mpl* publicitaires

advertising space
espace *m* publicitaire
advice note avis *m* d'expédition
affidavit déclaration *f* sous serment
after-sales service service *m* après-vente (SAV)
after-tax profit bénéfice *m* après impôts
agency agence *f*
agenda ordre du jour *m*
agent (n) représentant(e)
agree (approve) accepter, approuver; *(be same as)* concorder (avec)
agree to do sth. accepter de faire qch.
agreed price prix convenu
agreement contrat *m*, accord *m*
aim (n) objectif *m*, but *m*
aim (v) viser (à), avoir pour but (de)
air freight transport *m* par avion, fret aérien
air freight charges/rates tarifs *mpl* de transport par avion
airfreight (v) expédier par avion
airmail (n) poste *f* aérienne
airmail (v) envoyer par avion
airport aéroport *m*
airport tax taxe *m* d'aéroport
airtight packaging emballage *m* hermétique
all expenses paid tous frais payés
all-in price prix net, tarif tout compris
all-risks policy assurance *f* tous risques
allow 10% for carriage ajouter 10% pour le transport
allowance for depreciation provisions *fpl* pour dépréciation
amend rectifier, modifier, corriger
amendment modification *f*, amendement *m*, correction *f*
amortization amortissement *m*
amortize amortir, rembourser
amount (money) montant *m*, somme *f*
amount owing somme due
amount paid montant versé, versement *m*
amount to s'élever à, se monter à
analysis analyse *f*
annual accounts comptes annuels, comptes de l'exercice

annual general meeting (AGM) assemblée générale annuelle
annual report rapport annuel
annually annuellement, chaque année
answer (n) réponse *f*
answer the telephone répondre au téléphone
answering machine répondeur *m* téléphonique
answering service permanence *f* téléphonique
appeal (against a decision) (v) faire appel; (n) appel *m* (d'un jugement)
appeal to (v) *(attract)* attirer, séduire
appendix annexe *f*
application (for job, etc.) demande *f*
application form formulaire *m* de candidature/de demande (d'emploi)
apply for a job solliciter un emploi, poser sa candidature à un poste
apply to *(affect)* concerner
appoint nommer
appointment (job) poste *m*, emploi *m*; *(meeting)* rendez-vous *m*
appointments book carnet *m* de rendez-vous
appointments vacant offres *f* d'emploi
appreciate apprécier; *(in value)* augmenter en valeur, s'apprécier
appreciation appréciation *f*; *(in value)* augmentation *f* en valeur, appréciation *f*
approval, on à l'essai, à condition
approve the terms of a contract approuver les termes d'un contrat
approximate approximatif (-ive)
approximately environ, approximativement
arbitrate in a dispute arbitrer un conflit
arbitration board comité *m* de conciliation
area code *(tel.)* indicatif *m* de zone
area manager directeur (-trice) régional(e)
arrange (meeting) arranger, organiser
arrears arriéré *m*
article (clause) clause *f*; *(item)* article *m*

as per advice suivant avis
as per invoice conformément à la facture, selon la facture
as per sample selon échantillon, conformément à l'échantillon
ask (so. to do sth.) demander (à qqn de faire qch.)
ask for a refund demander un remboursement
ask for further details demander des renseignements supplémentaires
assess damages évaluer les dommages
assessment of damages évaluation des dommages
asset actif m, avoir m
asset value valeur f de l'actif
assist aider
assistant assistant(e) (n)
assistant manager directeur (-trice) adjoint(e)
associate (adj) associé(e)
associate (n) associé(e), collègue m/f
assurance assurance f
assurance policy police f d'assurance-vie
assure so.'s life assurer qqn sur la vie
attend (a meeting) assister à (une réunion)
attend to s'occuper de (qch.)
attorney fondé m de pouvoir
auction (n) enchère f, vente f aux enchères
auction (v) vendre aux enchères
audit (n) vérification f comptable, audit m
audit the accounts vérifier les comptes
auditor audit m, auditeur m, commissaire m aux comptes
authority autorité f
authorization autorisation f
authorize payment autoriser le paiement
availability disponibilité f
available disponible
average (adj) moyen(ne)
average (n) moyenne f
average price prix moyen
await instructions attendre les instructions
award a contract to so. donner/adjuger un contrat à qqn

B

back orders commandes en attente
back tax rappel m d'impôt
back up (v) (computer file) sauvegarder; (support) appuyer, étayer
backdate antidater
backlog travail m en retard/attente
backup copy disquette de sauvegarde
bad debt créance f douteuse
balance (n) solde m (d'un compte)
balance (v) a budget équilibrer un budget
balance brought down/forward solde m à nouveau, ancien solde, solde reporté
balance carried down/forward solde m à ce jour, solde à reporter
balance due to us, balance owing solde m à recevoir, solde à régler, dû m
balance of payments balance f des paiements
balance sheet bilan m
ban (n) interdiction f, embargo m
ban (v) interdire
bank (n) banque f
bank (v) (cheque/check) mettre à la banque; (have an account) avoir un compte bancaire (à/au)
bank account compte m bancaire
bank balance solde m en banque, position f d'un compte (bancaire)
bank base rate taux m de base bancaire
bank charges frais mpl bancaires, agios mpl
bank draft traite f bancaire
bank holiday jour m férié
bank statement relevé m de compte
bank transfer virement m bancaire
banker's order ordre m de virement bancaire
banknote billet m de banque
bankrupt (adj/n) failli(e)
bankrupt (v) causer/entraîner la faillite
bankruptcy faillite f
bar chart diagramme m en bâtons; histogramme m
bar code code m (à) barres

bargain

bargain (n) affaire f, occasion f; *(deal)* marché m, affaire f

bargain (v) discuter, marchander

bargaining position prise f de position dans les négociations

barter (n) troc m

barter (v) troquer

base (n) *(initial position)* base f

basic (adj) *(most important)* de base, essentiel (-elle)

basic discount remise f de base, remise habituelle

basic tax impôt m normal/de base

batch (n) *(of products)* lot m

batch (v) grouper

batch number numéro m de lot

bear (v) **(interest)** porter intérêt

bearer porteur m

begin commencer

behalf of, on au nom de

benchmark (point de) référence f, repère m

beneficiary bénéficiaire m/f, ayant droit m

benefit from (v) profiter de, bénéficier de

berth (v) accoster, mouiller, arriver à quai

bid (n) *(offer to buy)* offre f, mise f

bilateral bilatéral(e)

bill (n) *(in a restaurant)* addition f; *(list of charges)* facture f, note f

bill (v) facturer, présenter la facture

bill of exchange lettre f de change

bill of lading connaissement m

bill of sale contrat m/act m de vente

bills payable effets mpl à payer

bills receivable effets mpl à recevoir

black economy travail m au noir, économie f parallèle

black list (n) liste noire

black market marché m noir

blacklist (v) mettre sur la liste noire

blank cheque/check chèque m en blanc

block (v) bloquer

block booking réservation f en bloc

board (n) *(group of people)* conseil m, comité m

board meeting réunion f du conseil d'administration

board of directors conseil m d'administration; directoire m

bond *(government)* bon m (du Trésor), obligation f

bonus prime f

book (v) réserver

book value valeur f comptable

bookkeeper employé(e) aux écritures

bookkeeping comptabilité f, tenue f des livres

boom industry industrie f en pleine croissance/en pleine expansion

border frontière f

borrow emprunter

borrower emprunteur (-euse)

boss *(informal)* patron m

bottleneck goulot m/goulet m d'étranglement

bought ledger grand livre des achats

box number numéro m de boîte postale

bracket together grouper, réunir

branch succursale f, agence f *(d'une banque)*

branch manager directeur (-trice) de succursale/d'agence

brand marque f

brand loyalty fidélité f à la marque

brand name marque f, nom m de marque

breach of contract rupture f de contrat

break an agreement rompre un accord/un contrat

break down (v) *(itemize)* ventiler les frais; *(machine)* être en panne, avoir une panne

break even (v) rentrer dans ses frais

break off negotiations arrêter/rompre les négociations

break the law enfreindre la loi

breakdown (n) *(items)* détail m, ventilation f; *(machine)* panne f, défaillance f

breakeven point seuil m de rentabilité

bribe (n) pot-de-vin m

briefcase serviette f, porte-documents m

brochure brochure f

budget (n) budget m

budget (v) budgéter, budgétiser

budget account compte m crédit

budgetary control contrôle m budgétaire

built-in incorporé(e), intégré(e)
bulk buying achat en gros
business affaires fpl
business (company) entreprise f;
(discussion) question f, point m
business, on pour affaires
business address adresse f du
bureau/du lieu de travail
business class classe f affaires
business hours
heures fpl d'ouverture
business lunch déjeuner m d'affaires,
repas m d'affaires
business premises local m à usage
de bureaux; locaux mpl
commerciaux
business strategy
stratégie f des affaires
businessman/businesswoman
homme/femme d'affaires
busy occupé(e)
buy (v) acheter
buy forward acheter à terme
buyer (person) acheteur (-euse)
buying department service m achats

C

calculate calculer, estimer
calculation calcul m
calculator calculatrice f, calculette f
calendar month mois civil/complet
calendar year année civile
call (n) (phone) appel m téléphonique, communication f; (visit) visite f
call (v) (phone) téléphoner à qqn,
appeler qqn
call (v) **collect** appeler en PCV
call off a deal annuler/résilier un
contrat/une affaire
cancel annuler; décommander
cancel a contract
annuler/résilier un contrat
cancellation clause
clause f résolutoire
cancellation of an appointment
annulation f d'un rendez-vous
capacity (production) capacité f,
rendement m; (space) capacité f,
volume m
capital capital m, capitaux mpl
capital equipment
biens mpl d'équipement

capital expenditure (coût
d')acquisition f d'immobilisations
capital gains plus-value f
capitalization capitalisation f
capitalize doter en capital, capitaliser
capitalize on profiter de, exploiter
captive market marché m captif
capture prendre le contrôle (de)
card carte f (professionnelle)
card index (n) fichier m
card phone téléphone m à carte
cardboard box
boîte f en carton, carton m
care of (c/o) aux bons soins de/chez
cargo (goods) cargaison f
carriage transport m, port m
carriage forward port dû, en port dû
carriage free franc(o) de port
carriage paid port payé, en port payé
carrier (company) transporteur m,
entreprise f de transports
carry (have in stock) avoir en stock;
(transport) porter, transporter
carry forward reporter
carton boîte f en carton, carton m
case (n) (box) caisse f
cash (n) (money) argent m
comptant, espèces fpl,
liquide m, cash m
cash a cheque/check
toucher/ encaisser un chèque
cash advance avance f de caisse
cash balance solde m de trésorerie
cash book livre m de caisse
cash card carte f de retrait
cash discount escompte m de caisse
cash flow marge f brute d'auto-
financement (MBA); flux m de
trésorerie
cash flow forecast
prévisions fpl de trésorerie
cash offer offre f en espèces,
offre au comptant
cash on delivery (c.o.d.) paiement m
à la livraison, livraison f contre
remboursement
cash price prix m du comptant
cash purchase
achat m (au) comptant
cash sale vente f au comptant
cash terms paiement m comptant
casting vote voix f prépondérante
casual work travail m temporaire

catalogue/catalog catalogue m
catalogue/catalog price
prix m catalogue
cater for fournir
caveat emptor aux risques de
l'acheteur
ceiling price prix m plafond
cellular telephone
téléphone m cellulaire
central bank banque f centrale
central purchasing
achats mpl centralisés
centralize centraliser
certificate of approval certificat m
d'homologation
certificate of deposit certificat m de
dépôt, bon de caisse
certificate of origin
certificat m d'origine
certified cheque/check
chèque certifié
certified copy
copie certifiée conforme
certify certifier
chain store
magasin m à succursales multiples
chairman (company) président(e)
chairman and managing director
président-directeur m
général (PDG)
Chamber of Commerce Chambre f
de Commerce
change (n) (cash) monnaie f;
(difference) changement m
change (v) changer
change hands
changer de propriétaire
channels of distribution canaux mpl
de distribution
charge (n) (money) prix m, droit m,
frais mpl
charge (v) (money) demander, faire
payer, facturer
charge card carte f accréditive
charter flight vol m charter
chase (an order) relancer, activer
cheap bon marché
cheap labour/labor main-d'œuvre f
bon marché
cheap rate tarif m réduit
check (n) (examination)
contrôle m, vérification f
check (v) (examine) vérifier

check in (airport) se présenter à
l'enregistrement; (hotel) arriver à
l'hôtel, s'inscrire à l'arrivée
check-in (airport) enregistrement m
check-in counter enregistrement m
check-in time
heure f d'enregistrement
check out (hotel) quitter l'hôtel;
régler la note d'hôtel au départ
checkout (supermarket) caisse f
cheque/check chèque m
cheque/check book carnet m de
chèques, chéquier m
cheque/check number
numéro m de chèque
chief (adj) principal(e)
chief executive officer (CEO)
président-directeur m
général (PDG)
choice (n) (of items) choix m
choose choisir
Christmas bonus treizième mois
circular (n) circulaire f
circular letter of credit lettre f de
crédit circulaire
claim (n) réclamation f, demande f,
revendication f
claim (v) (insurance) réclamer (des
dommages-intérêts)
claims department service m des
sinistres/des réclamations
classified advertisements annonces
classées, petites annonces
classified directory répertoire m
d'adresses par professions
classify classer
clause clause f, article m
clear (adj) (understandable) clair(e)
clear (v) (stock) liquider
clear a cheque/check
compenser un chèque
clear profit bénéfice m net
clearing bank
banque f de compensation
clerical error erreur f d'écriture
clerk employé(e) de bureau
client client(e)
clientele clientèle f
clinch (a deal) conclure (un accord)
close a meeting lever la séance
close an account fermer/clôturer
un compte
close down fermer

closed fermé(e)
closed market marché d'exclusivité
closing balance
  bilan *m* de fin d'exercice
closing date date *f* limite
closing price
  prix *m*/cours *m* de clôture
closing stock
  stock *m* en fin d'exercice
closing time heure *f* de fermeture
co-operate collaborer, coopérer
co-operation coopération *f*
co-opt so. coopter qqn
code of practice politique *f* générale
  (de l'entreprise)
cold call visite impromptue
  (d'un représentant)
cold store chambre *f* froide,
  entrepôt *m* frigorifique
collaborate collaborer
collaboration collaboration *f*
collapse (n) effondrement *m*
collapse (v) s'effondrer, s'écrouler
collateral (n)
  garantie *f*, nantissement *m*
collect (v) *(fetch)* aller chercher
collect a debt recouvrer une créance
collect call appel *m* en PCV
collection *(of goods)* enlèvement *m*
collective ownership
  propriété *f* collective
collector percepteur *m*, receveur *m*
commerce commerce *m*
commercial (adj) commercial(e)
commercial (n) *(TV)* publicité *f*, pub *f*,
  spot *m* publicitaire (à la télévision)
commercial law droit *m* commercial
commission *(money)* commission *f*
commission rep
  représentant *m* à la commission
commodity marchandise *f*, denrée *f*
commodity exchange bourse *f* de
  commerce/des matières premières
commodity market marché *m* des
  matières premières
common pricing fixation *f* concertée
  des prix
communicate communiquer
communications communications *fpl*
company société *f*, compagnie *f*
company director directeur (-trice)
comparable comparable
compare comparer

compare with être comparable à
comparison comparaison *f*
compensate *(for loss)*
  dédommager, indemniser
compensation *(for loss)*
  dédommagement *m*,
  indemnisation *f*
competing products
  produits *mpl* concurrentiels
competition concurrence *f*
competitive price prix *m*
  concurrentiel, prix compétitif
competitive products
  produits *mpl* concurrentiels
competitiveness compétitivité *f*
competitor concurrent(e)
complain (about) se plaindre (de)
complaint réclamation *f*
complaints department service *m*
  des réclamations
complete complet (-ète), achevé(e)
complete (v) exécuter, terminer
complimentary ticket billet *m* gratuit,
  billet de faveur
comply with se conformer à
compound interest
  intérêts *mpl* composés
comprehensive insurance
  assurance *f* tous risques
compromise (n) compromis *m*
compromise (v)
  arriver à un compromis
compulsory obligatoire
compulsory purchase *(of land)*
  expropriation *f*
computer ordinateur *m*
computer error erreur *f* faite par
  l'ordinateur, erreur d'ordinateur
computer file fichier *m*
computer printout sortie *f*
  d'imprimante, listing *m*
computer program
  programme *m*, logiciel *m*
computer system
  système *m* informatique
computer terminal
  terminal *m* d'ordinateur
computerize informatiser
concern (v) *(deal with)* concerner
conclude *(agreement)* conclure
condition *(state)* condition *f*, état *m*
condition *(terms)* condition *f*

condition that, on à (la) condition que, sous réserve de

conditional conditionnel (-elle)

conditions of employment conditions fpl d'emploi

conditions of sale conditions fpl de vente

conduct negotiations mener des négociations

conference phone téléphone m de conférence

conference room salle f de conférences/de réunion

confidential confidentiel (-elle)

confirm a booking confirmer une réservation

confirmation confirmation f

conflict of interest conflit m d'intérêts

connecting flight correspondance f

connection lien m, relation f

consignment (sending) expédition f, envoi m

consignment (things received) arrivage m; (things sent) envoi m

consignment note bordereau m d'expédition

consist of consister en, comprendre

consolidate (shipments) grouper

consortium consortium m

constant constant(e)

consult consulter

consultancy firm cabinet-conseil m

consultant expert m, consultant m

consumer consommateur (-trice)

consumer goods biens mpl de consommation

consumer research recherche f des besoins des consommateurs

contact (n) (person) relation f, contact m

contact (v) contacter, joindre

contain contenir

container (box, tin) récipient m, contenant m

container (for shipping) conteneur m

container terminal terminal m maritime (pour porte-conteneurs)

containerization conteneurisation m, mise f en conteneurs

containerize conteneuriser, mettre (des marchandises) en conteneurs

contents contenu m

contingency plan plan m d'urgence

continual continuel (-elle)

continually continuellement, sans cesse

continue continuer

continuous continu(e)

contra account compte m de contrepartie

contra an entry contrepasser une écriture

contra entry écriture f de contrepartie, contrepassation f

contract (n) contrat m, engagement m

contract (v) contracter

contract note avis m d'exécution

contract of employment contrat m de travail

contractor entrepreneur m, entreprise f

contractual liability responsabilité f contractuelle

contractually conformément à un contrat

contrary contraire

control (n) (check) contrôle m, vérification f, surveillance f; (power) contrôle m, maîtrise f

control a business diriger une entreprise

control key touche f de contrôle

convene convoquer

convenient pratique, commode

conversion price/rate taux m de conversion

convert changer de l'argent

convertible loan stock valeurs f convertibles

cooling off period (after purchase) délai m de réflexion

copy (n) (of document) copie f

copy (v) faire une copie, reproduire

corner the market accaparer le marché

corporate image image f de marque

corporate plan plan m de développement de la société

corporate profits bénéfices mpl d'une société

corporation société f

corporation tax
impôt m sur les sociétés

correspond with so. *(write)*
correspondre avec qqn

correspondence correspondance f

cost (n) coût m, frais mpl, prix m

cost (v) coûter, valoir

cost analysis analyse f des coûts

cost centre centre m de coût

cost, insurance and freight (c.i.f.)
coût, assurance, fret (CAF)

cost of living coût m de la vie

cost of sales coût m de revient (des
marchandises vendues)

cost plus coût m majoré

cost price prix m coûtant

cost-effective rentable

cost-effectiveness rentabilité f

cost-of-living allowance indemnité f
de vie chère

cost-of-living index indice m du coût
de la vie

counter comptoir m, rayon m

counter-claim (n)
demande f reconventionnelle

counter-claim (v) opposer une
demande reconventionnelle

counter-offer contre-proposition f

counterfoil talon m, souche f

countermand annuler

countersign contresigner

country of origin pays m d'origine

coupon ad
publicité f avec coupon-réponse

courier *(guide)* accompagnateur
(-trice); *(messenger)* coursier m

court cour f, tribunal m

covenant (n) engagement m

cover (n) *(insurance)*
garantie f, couverture f

cover a risk
être assuré contre un risque

cover costs
couvrir les coûts de production

cover note
attestation f provisoire d'assurance

covering letter
lettre f d'accompagnement

credit (n) crédit m

credit (v) créditer un compte

credit account compte m crédit

credit balance solde m créditeur

credit card sale vente f réglée par
carte de crédit

credit control contrôle m de crédit,
encadrement m du crédit

credit entry écriture f au crédit

credit facilities facilités fpl de crédit

credit freeze restriction f/
encadrement m du crédit

credit limit
plafond m/limite f de crédit

credit note facture f d'avoir, note f
de crédit

credit transfer virement m de crédit

credit, on à crédit

creditor créancier m

crossed cheque/check chèque barré

cumulative cumulatif (-ive)

cumulative interest
intérêts mpl composés

currency devise f (étrangère)

current account compte m courant

current assets actif m circulant

current liabilities dettes fpl à court
terme, passif m exigible

current rate of exchange taux m de
change en vigueur

curriculum vitae (CV)
curriculum m vitae (CV)

customer client(e)

customer satisfaction satisfaction f
du client

customer service department
service m clients

customs douane f

customs clearance dédouanement m

customs declaration form formulaire m de déclaration en douane

customs duty droit m de douane

customs entry point
poste m frontière

customs official douanier m

cut (n) réduction f

cut (v) réduire, diminuer, supprimer

cut price (n) prix m réduit

cut-price goods marchandises à
prix sacrifiés

cycle cycle m

cyclical cyclique

cyclical factors
facteurs mpl conjoncturels

damage

D

damage (n) dommage m, dégâts mpl
damage (v) abîmer, endommager
damages dommages-intérêts mpl, dommages et intérêts
data données fpl
database base f de données
date (n) date f
date (v) dater
date stamp cachet m de la poste; timbre m dateur
day (24 hours) jour m; (working day) jour m, journée f (de travail)
dead account compte m oisif, compte qui dort
deadline date f limite
deadlock (n) impasse f
deadlock (v) arriver à une impasse
deal marché m, accord m, contrat m
deal in (v) faire le commerce de
deal with an order s'occuper d'une/ exécuter une commande
dealer négociant(e), marchand(e)
dear (expensive) cher (chère), coûteux (-euse)
debenture obligation f (non garantie)
debit (n) débit m
debit an account débiter un compte
debit entry écriture f au débit
debit note note f de débit
debt dette f
debt collection recouvrement m de dettes
debt collection agency agence f de recouvrement (de dettes)
debt, in endetté(e)
debtor débiteur m
decide on a course of action arrêter un plan d'action
deciding factor facteur m décisif
decimal point virgule f (décimale)
declare goods to customs déclarer des marchandises à la douane
declared value valeur f déclarée
decrease (n) baisse f, diminution f
decrease (v) baisser, diminuer
decrease in value diminution f/ perte f de valeur
decreasing décroissant(e), en baisse
deduct déduire, retrancher, prélever
deductible déductible

deduction déduction f, prélèvement m, retenue f
deed acte m
default (n) manquement m, défaillance f
default on payments se trouver en cessation de paiements
defaulter défaillant(e)
defect défaut m, vice m de fabrication
defective (faulty) défectueux (-euse)
defer payment différer le paiement
deferment of payment délai m de paiement
deferred creditor créancier m différé
deficit déficit m
deficit financing financement m du déficit budgétaire
defray (costs) défrayer/couvrir (des frais)
delay (n) retard m
delay (v) être en retard, retarder
delete rayer, supprimer
deliver livrer
delivered price prix tout compris (port et emballage inclus)
delivery (goods) livraison f, envoi m
delivery date date m de livraison
delivery note bulletin m de livraison
delivery time délai m de livraison
demand (n) (payment) demande f, réclamation f; (need) demande f
demand (v) réclamer
demonstrate faire une démonstration
demonstration model modèle m/ appareil m de démonstration
department (in office) service m, bureau m; (in shop) rayon m
department store grand magasin
depend on dépendre de, compter sur
depending on suivant, en fonction de
deposit (n) (in bank) dépôt m; (paid in advance) acompte m, provision f, arrhes fpl
deposit (v) déposer/verser de l'argent (sur un compte)
deposit account compte m de dépôt(s), compte sur livret
deposit slip bordereau m de versement
depositor déposant(e)

depreciate *(lose value)* diminuer de valeur, se déprécier
depreciation *(loss of value)* moins-value f, dévaluation f
depreciation rate taux m d'amortissement
deputize for assurer l'intérim de
deputy suppléant(e), adjoint(e)
deputy manager directeur (-trice) adjoint(e)
deputy managing director directeur (-trice) général(e) adjoint(e)
design (n) étude f, design m
design (v) dessiner, concevoir
design department bureau m d'études
desk bureau m
desk-top publishing publication f assistée par ordinateur (PAO)
destination destination f
detail (n) détail m, précision f
detailed account compte m détaillé
devaluation dévaluation f
devalue dévaluer
diagram diagramme m, schéma m, graphique m
dial a number composer un numéro
dialling code indicatif m
differ différer
direct (adj) direct(e)
direct (v) diriger, mener
direct debit prélèvement m automatique
direct mail publicité f directe
direct tax impôt m direct
directions for use mode m d'emploi
director directeur (-trice); *(non-executive)* administrateur (-trice)
directory répertoire m d'adresses
disclaimer déni m de responsabilité
disclose a piece of information divulguer un renseignement
disclosure of confidential information divulgation f de renseignements confidentiels
discontinue cesser
discount (n) réduction f, remise f, escompte m, rabais m
discount (v) vendre au rabais
discount price prix avec rabais
discounted cash flow (DCF) cash-flow actualisé
discrepancy erreur f, écart m

discuss discuter
discussion discussion f
disk disque m
disk drive lecteur m disques/ de disquettes
dismiss licencier
dismissal licenciement m
dispatch (n) *(sending)* envoi m, expédition f
dispatch (v) *(send)* expédier
dispatch note bordereau m d'expédition
display (n) présentation f, étalage m
display (v) présenter
display material matériel m publicitaire
display stand présentoir m, étalage m
disposable à jeter après usage
disposal vente f
dispose of excess stock écouler le surplus de stock
distress sale vente f forcée
distribute distribuer
distribution distribution f; *(books)* diffusion f
distribution costs frais mpl de distribution/de diffusion
distribution manager responsable m/f de la distribution/de la diffusion
distributor concessionnaire m, distributeur m; *(books)* diffuseur m
diversification diversification f
diversify diversifier, varier
dividend dividende m
dividend yield taux m de rendement d'une action
division *(company)* division f, secteur m
dock (n) bassin m
dock (v) arriver à quai, accoster
documentation documentation f
dollar dollar m (américain)
dollar balance balance f commerciale en dollars
domestic market marché m intérieur
domestic production production f intérieure
domestic sales ventes fpl intérieures
door-to-door selling démarchage m, porte-à-porte

dossier dossier *m*
double (v) doubler
double taxation double imposition *f*
double-booking
  surréservation *f*, surbooking *m*
down payment acompte *m*
down-market (de) bas de gamme
downside factor facteur *m*
  pessimiste/négatif
downturn repli *m*, baisse *f*, recul *m*
draft plan esquisse *f*, plan *m*
draft (n) *(money)* traite *f*, lettre *f* de
  change; *(rough plan)* esquisse *f*,
  ébauche *f*, avant-projet *m*
draft a contract
  faire une ébauche de contrat
draw a cheque/check tirer un chèque
draw up a contract
  rédiger un contrat
drawee tiré *m*
drawer tireur *m*
drop (n) chute *f*, baisse *f*
drop (v) baisser, chuter
drop in sales chute *f* des ventes
dud cheque/check
  chèque *m* sans provision
due *(awaited)* attendu(e);
  (owing) dû, due
dues commandes *fpl* anticipées
dummy maquette *f*
dummy pack emballage *m* factice,
  boîte *f* factice
dump goods on a market
  faire du dumping
dumping dumping *m*
duplicate (n)
  double *m*, duplicata *m*, copie *f*
duplicate (v) polycopier
duty *(tax)* taxe *f*, droit *m*
duty-free hors taxe, exempt de droits

E

earmark funds for a project affecter
  des fonds à un projet
earn *(interest)* rapporter;
  (money) gagner, mériter
earnings *(profit)* gain *m*, bénéfice *m*;
  (salary) salaire *m*, revenu(s) *mpl*
easy terms facilités *fpl* de paiement
economic cycle cycle *m* économique
economic development
  développement *m* économique

economic growth
  croissance *f* économique
economic indicators
  indicateurs *mpl* économiques
economic trends tendances *fpl*
  économiques, conjoncture *f*
  économique
economical
  économique, avantageux (-euse)
economies of scale
  économies d'échelle
economize économiser,
  faire des économies
economy *(saving)* économie *f*
economy class *(in plane)*
  classe touriste
ecu/ECU (European currency unit)
  écu/ECU *m*
effect (n) résultat *m*, effet *m*
effect (v) effectuer
effective efficace
effective yield rendement *m* effectif
effectiveness efficacité *f*
efficiency efficacité *f*, performance *f*
efficient efficace, compétent(e)
electronic mail/e-mail
  courrier *m* électronique
electronic point of sale (EPOS)
  point *m* de vente électronique
embargo (n) embargo *m*
embargo (v) mettre l'embargo sur
embark embarquer, monter à bord
embark on entreprendre
employ employer
employee employé(e), salarié(e)
employer employeur *m*
employment emploi *m*
enclose joindre
enclosure (encl.) pièce *f* jointe (p.j.)
end (n) fin *f*
end (v) prendre fin, finir, se terminer
end of season sale vente *f* de fin
  de saison
end product produit *m* fini
end user utilisateur *m*,
  consommateur *m* (final)
endorse a cheque/check endosser
  un chèque
endorsement endossement *m*;
  (on insurance) avenant *m*
energy-saving (adj)
  qui économise l'énergie

engaged *(telephone)* occupé(e)
enter *(go in)* entrer, pénétrer; *(write in)* inscrire, enregistrer, noter
enter into *(discussion)* entamer
enterprise entreprise *f*
entitle autoriser, donner à qqn le droit de
entitlement droit *m*
entrepreneur entrepreneur *m*
entry *(going in)* entrée *f*; *(writing)* écriture *f*
entry visa visa *m* d'entrée
equip équiper
equipment équipement *m*, matériel *m*
equities actions *fpl* ordinaires
equity capital capitaux *mpl* propres
error erreur *f*
errors and omissions excepted (e. & o.e.) sauf erreur ou omission
escape clause clause échappatoire
escrow account compte bloqué
establish établir, ouvrir, fonder
establishment *(business)* maison *f* de commerce, établissement *m*
estimate (n) *(calculation)* évaluation *f*, estimation *f*; *(quote)* devis *m*
estimate (v) estimer
estimated sales estimation *f* des ventes
Eurocheque eurochèque *m*
European Union (EU) Union européenne (UE)
evaluate costs évaluer les coûts
evaluation évaluation *f*
exact exact(e)
examination *(inspection)* examen *m*, contrôle *m*
examine examiner
exceed excéder, dépasser
excellent excellent(e)
excess capacity surcapacité *f*
excessive excessif (-ive), démesuré(e)
exchange (n) *(currency)* change *m*
exchange (v) échanger; *(currency)* changer de l'argent
exchange rate taux *m* de change
excise duty droits *mpl* de régie
excluding à l'exception de
exclusion clause clause *f* d'exclusion
exclusive agreement contrat *m* d'exclusivité
exclusive of tax hors taxe
exclusivity exclusivité *f*
executive (adj) exécutif (-ive)
executive (n) directeur (-trice), dirigeant *m*, cadre *m*
exempt (adj) exempté(e), exonéré(e)
exempt (v) exempter, exonérer
exempt from tax exonéré(e) d'impôt
exemption from tax exonération *f* d'impôt
exercise an option lever une option
exercise of an option levée *f* d'une option
exhibit (v) exposer
exhibition exposition *f*
exhibitor exposant *m*
expand augmenter, (se) développer
expenditure dépense *f*
expense dépense *f*, frais *mpl*
expense account note *f* de frais, frais *mpl* de représentation
expensive cher (-ère), coûteux (-euse)
experienced expérimenté(e), compétent(e)
expire expirer, prendre fin, venir à expiration
expiry terminaison *f*, expiration *f*
expiry date date d'expiration
export (n) exportation *f*, export *m*
export (v) exporter
export department service *m* des exportations, service export
export licence/permit licence *f*/ permis *m* d'exportation
export manager chef *m* du service export
exporter exportateur *m*, société *f* exportatrice
exports exportations *fpl*, marchandises *fpl* exportées
exposure risque *m*
express (adj) *(fast)* rapide, exprès
express delivery livraison *f* exprès
extend *(make longer)* prolonger
extended credit crédit *m* à long terme
extension *(making longer)* prolongation *f*; *(telephone)* poste *m* (téléphonique)
external audit audit *m* externe

external auditor auditeur *m* externe
external trade
commerce *m* extérieur
extra charges supplément *m*,
frais *mpl* supplémentaires
extras *(expenses)*
frais *mpl* supplémentaires

F

face value valeur nominale
facilities installations *fpl*; locaux *mpl*
factor (n) *(influence)* facteur *m*
factor (n) *(person, company)*
factor *m*, société *f* d'affacturage/
de factoring
factoring charges
commission *f* d'affacturage
factors of production
facteurs *mpl* de production
factory usine *f*, fabrique *f*
factory price prix *m* départ usine
fail *(go bust)* faire faillite; *(not to
succeed)* échouer
failing that à défaut, sinon
failure *(of machine)* panne *f*, arrêt *m*
fair (adj) honnête, correct(e)
fair price prix raisonnable/équitable
fair wear and tear usure *f* normale
faked documents documents *mpl*,
papiers falsifiés
fall behind *(worse position)* se laisser
distancer; *(late)* être en retard,
prendre du retard
fall due venir à échéance;
arriver à maturité
fall through
échouer, ne pas avoir lieu
false pretences
moyens *mpl* frauduleux
farm out work sous-traiter
fast-selling items articles qui se
vendent rapidement
favourable/favorable balance of trade
balance *f* commerciale bénéficiaire
fax (n) fax *m*, télécopie *f*
fax (v) envoyer par fax/par télécopie
feasibility report
rapport *m* de faisabilité
fee *(admission)* droit *m* (d'entrée);
(for services) honoraires *mpl*,
rémunération *f*
figure chiffre *m*; total *m*, montant *m*

figures chiffres *mpl*;
résultat *m* quantitatif
file (n) *(computer)* fichier *m*;
(documents) dossier *m*
file documents
classer (des documents)
filing cabinet classeur *m*
fill a gap combler un manque
final demand dernier rappel
finalize mettre au point
finance (n) finance *f*
finance (v) financer
finance director directeur financier
finances argent *m*, finances *fpl*
financial financier (-ière)
financial position position *f*/
situation *f* financière
financial resources
ressources *fpl* financières
financial risk risque *m* financier
financial year exercice *m* financier
financing financement *m*
fine (n) amende *f*
fine (v)
condamner qqn à une amende
fire damage dégâts *mpl* causés par
le feu
fire insurance assurance *f* incendie,
assurance contre l'incendie
firm (n) firme *f*, maison *f*,
société *f*, entreprise *f*
firm price prix *m* ferme
first in first out (FIFO) *(accounting)*
premier entré, premier sorti
(PEPS)
first option en première option
first-class *(goods)*
de première qualité
fiscal measures mesures *fpl* fiscales
fix *(mend)* réparer
fix a meeting for 3 p.m. fixer une
réunion à 15h
fixed costs coûts *mpl* fixes
fixed income revenu *m* fixe
fixed scale of charges barème *m* fixe,
échelle *f* de prix fixe
fixed-price agreement contrat *m*
forfaitaire, contrat à prix
fixed-term contract
contrat à durée déterminée
flat rate taux *m* fixe, forfait *m*
flexibility souplesse *f*, flexibilité *f*
flexible souple, adaptable, flexible

flight of capital fuite f de capitaux
flip chart
  tableau m à feuilles mobiles
float (n) *(cash)* caisse f; *(cash advance)* avance f (de caisse)
float (v) *(a currency)* laisser flotter
float a company lancer une société (en Bourse)
floating exchange rates taux de change flottants
floor *(level)* étage m
floor plan plan m d'ensemble
floor space surface f au sol
flop (n) échec m, ratage m, fiasco m
flop (v) échouer, rater
flotation lancement m d'une société en Bourse
flourishing prospère, florissant(e)
flow-chart/diagram
  organigramme m (de production)
fluctuate fluctuer, osciller
fluctuation fluctuation f
follow-up letter lettre f de relance
for sale à vendre
force majeure force f majeure
forced sale liquidation f forcée, vente f forcée
forecast (n) prévisions fpl
forecast (v) prévoir
foreign currency devises fpl
foreign exchange *(currency)* change m
foreign money order mandat m international
forfeit a deposit perdre des arrhes
forfeiture confiscation f (d'un bien)
fork-lift truck chariot m élévateur
form (n) formulaire m
form of words énoncé m, formulation f
formal officiel (-elle)
forward buying achat m à terme
forward market marché m à terme
forward rate taux m de change à terme
forwarding address adresse f de réexpédition
forwarding instructions instructions relatives à l'expédition
franc *(currency)* franc m
franchise (n) franchise f
franchise (v)
  accorder une franchise, franchiser

franchisee franchisé m
franchiser franchiseur m
franchising franchisage m
franking machine machine f à affranchir
fraud fraude f
free (adj) *(no payment)* gratuit(e); *(no restrictions)* libre; *(not busy)* libre
free (adv) *(no payment)* gratuitement, sans payer
free delivery livraison gratuite, colis expédié franc de port
free of tax exonéré(e) d'impôt
free on board (f.o.b.) franco à bord (FAB)
free sample échantillon m gratuit
free trade zone zone franche
freeze (v) *(prices)* bloquer, geler
freight *(carriage)* fret m, prix m du transport
freight costs port m, frais mpl de transport
freight forward (en) port dû
freight plane avion-cargo m
frequent fréquent(e)
frozen account compte m gelé
frozen assets actifs mpl gelés, fonds mpl bloqués
fulfil an order exécuter une commande
full plein(e), complet (-ète)
full price prix m fort
full refund remboursement m total
full-time à temps complet, à plein temps
fund (n) fonds mpl
fund (v) financer
further to suite à, en réponse à
futures opérations fpl à terme

G

gain (n) *(size)* accroissement m, augmentation f; *(value)* augmentation f
gap in the market créneau m sur le marché
gearing effet m de levier, ratio m fonds propres/emprunts
general général(e)
general insurance assurance f multirisque

general manager
directeur (-trice) général(e)

general strike grève f générale

gentleman's agreement
gentleman's agreement m

genuine purchaser
acheteur m sérieux

get rid of sth. se débarrasser de qch.

gift cadeau m

gift voucher bon-cadeau m,
chèque-cadeau m

give *(as gift)* offrir

glut (n) surplus m, surabondance f

go into business se lancer dans
les affaires

going rate tarif en vigueur

good buy bonne affaire

good quality bonne qualité

good value *(for money)* aubaine f,
rapport qualité, prix excellent

goods marchandises fpl

goodwill goodwill m

government bonds
bons mpl du Trésor

government contractor
fournisseur m du gouvernement

graduate trainee
stagiaire m/f diplômé(e)

graduated income tax
impôt m progressif

gram/gramme gramme m

grand total total m général,
somme f globale

gratis gratis, gratuitement

gross (n) *(144)* douze douzaines,
grosse f

gross (v) rapporter brut, faire un
profit brut

gross domestic product (GDP)
produit m intérieur brut (PIB)

gross national product (GNP) produit
m national brut (PNB)

gross profit bénéfice m brut

gross salary salaire m brut

gross weight poids m brut

growth croissance f

growth rate taux m de croissance

guarantee (n) garantie f

guarantee (v) garantir

guideline ligne f de conduite, ligne
directrice, directive f

H

half (n) moitié f, demie f

half-price sale solde m à moitié prix

half-year semestre m comptable

hand luggage bagages mpl à main

hand over remettre

handle (v) *(deal with)*
s'occuper de, traiter

handling charges
frais mpl de manutention

handwritten
écrit(e) à la main, manuscrit(e)

harbour/harbor port m

hard bargain affaire f difficile

hard currency devise f forte

hard disk disque m dur

harmonization harmonisation f

haulage costs/rates frais mpl de
transport (routier)

head of department
chef m de service

head office siège m social,
bureau m central

headquarters (HQ) siège m social

heavy costs/expenditure
frais mpl importants

heavy equipment matériel m lourd

heavy goods vehicle (HGV)
poids lourd m

hectare hectare m

hidden asset bien m masqué

hidden reserves caisse f noire,
réserves fpl occultes

high interest intérêt m élevé

high rent loyer m élevé

high-quality de première qualité

highly-paid
qui perçoit un salaire élevé

highly-priced onéreux (-euse),
coûteux (-euse)

hire a car louer une voiture

hire purchase (HP)
achat m à crédit/à tempérament

hire staff embaucher du personnel

historical figures
chiffres mpl d'origine

hold (n) *(aircraft)* soute f; *(ship)* cale f

hold (v) *(contain)* contenir

hold a meeting/a discussion tenir
une réunion/une discussion

hold over remettre, ajourner

hold up (v) *(delay)* retarder

hold-up (n) *(delay)* retard *m*
holding company holding *m*
home address adresse *f* personnelle
home sales ventes *fpl* intérieures
honour/honor a bill
  honorer/acquitter une traite
hotel bill note *f* d'hôtel
hour heure *f*
hourly rate tarif *m* horaire
hourly wage salaire *m* horaire
hourly-paid workers
  ouvriers payés à l'heure
house *(company)* maison *f*, firme *f*
house insurance
  assurance-habitation *f*
hurry up (an order) activer/accélérer
  (une commande)

I

illegal illégal(e)
illegally illégalement
immediate immédiat(e)
immediately
  tout de suite, immédiatement
imperfect défectueux (-euse), de
  second choix
implement (n) outil *m*, instrument *m*
implement an agreement appliquer
  un accord
implementation
  exécution *f*, application *f*
import (n) importation *f*, import *m*
import (v) importer
import duty taxe *f* à l'importation
import licence/permit
  licence *f* d'importation
import quota contingent *m*/quota *m*
  d'importation
import-export import-export
importer importateur (-trice)
imports importations *fpl*
impulse buyer acheteur(-euse)
  impulsif(-ive)
in-house dans l'entreprise, dans
  la maison
incentive incitation *f*
incidental expenses faux frais *mpl*
include inclure, comprendre
inclusive inclus(e), compris(e)
inclusive charge tarif *m* tout compris
inclusive of tax taxe *f* comprise,
  toutes taxes comprises (TTC)

income revenu *m*
income tax impôt *m* sur le revenu
incoming call appel *m* de l'extérieur
incorporate (a company) constituer
  (une société)
incorrect incorrect(e)
incorrectly incorrectement
increase (n) augmentation *f*, hausse *f*
increase (v) **(the price of an item)**
  augmenter (le prix d'un article)
increase (v) **in price** augmenter de
  prix, coûter/être plus cher (-ère)
incur (costs) engager (des dépenses)
incur debts contracter des dettes
indebted qui a une dette envers qqn
indemnification indemnisation *f*,
  dédommagement *m*
indemnify so. for a loss indemniser
  qqn d'une perte
indemnity indemnité *f*
index (n) **(of prices)** indice *m*
  (des prix)
index (v) indexer
index-linked indexé(e)
indexation indexation *f*
indicator indicateur *m*
indirect taxation imposition *f*
  indirecte, impôts *mpl* indirects
induction courses/training
  cours *mpl* d'initiation
industrial (arbitration) tribunal
  conseil *m* de prud'hommes
industrial accident
  accident *m* du travail
industrial espionage
  espionnage *m* industriel
industrial relations relations *fpl* entre
  employeurs et employés
industrialist industriel *m*
industry *(companies)* industrie *f*
inefficiency inefficacité *f*;
  (human) incompétence *f*
inefficient inefficace;
  (human) incompétent(e)
inflation inflation *f*
inflationary inflationniste
influence (n) influence *f*
influence (v) influencer
information renseignement(s) *m(pl)*
infrastructure infrastructure *f*
infringe a patent contrefaire un
  produit protégé par un brevet

infringement of patent contrefaçon f (d'un produit breveté)
initial (v)
  parapher, signer de ses initiales
initial capital capital m initial, capital d'investissement
initiate discussions
  entamer des discussions
initiative initiative f
input information (computer)
  saisir/introduire des données
inquire se renseigner
inquiry demande f (officielle); demande de reseignement(s)
insolvent insolvable
inspect inspecter, vérifier, contrôler
inspection inspection f, vérification f, contrôle m
instalment versement m
instant credit crédit m immédiat
institution institution f
institutional investors
  investisseurs mpl institutionnels
instrument (document) acte m, document m, instrument m
insurance assurance f
insurance broker
  courtier m d'assurances
insurance company
  compagnie f d'assurances
insurance policy police f d'assurance
insure assurer
intangible assets
  immobilisations fpl incorporelles
interest (n) (on investment) intérêt m
interest (v) intéresser (qqn)
interest charges intérêts mpl (à payer), frais mpl financiers
interest rate taux m d'intérêt
interest-free credit crédit gratuit
interface (n) interface f
interim payment paiement m intérimaire, acompte m
intermediary intermédiaire m
internal audit audit m interne
international call appel m (téléphonique) international
international law
  droit m international
international trade
  commerce m international
interpret (v) interpréter, servir d'interprète

interpreter interprète m/f
interview (n) (for a job) entretien m
interview (v) (so. for a job) avoir un entretien avec (un candidat)
introduce présenter
introductory offer
  offre f de lancement
inventory (n) (list of contents) inventaire m; (stock) stock m
inventory control contrôle m des stocks, gestion f des stocks
invest faire un investissement, investir, placer (de l'argent)
investment investissement m, placement m (financier)
investment income
  revenus mpl de placements
invisible earnings revenus invisibles
invisible trade commerce m invisible
invite inviter qqn à, demander à qqn de
invoice (n) facture f, note f
invoice (v) facturer; envoyer une facture
invoice number numéro m de facture
invoice value/price prix m de facture
irrecoverable debt
  dette f irrécouvrable
irredeemable bond
  obligation f non remboursable
irregularities irrégularités fpl
irrevocable letter of credit lettre f de crédit irrévocable
issue a letter of credit émettre une lettre de crédit
issue instructions
  donner des instructions
item (on the agenda) question f (à l'ordre du jour)
item (thing for sale) article m
itemized account compte m détaillé
itemized invoice facture f détaillée

J

job (employment) emploi m, travail m; (piece of work) travail m, tâche f
job description description f de la fonction, profil m de poste
job security sécurité f de l'emploi
job title titre m, qualification f

join joindre, relier

joint account compte *m* joint

joint managing director codirecteur (-trice) général(e), directeur (-trice) général(e) adjoint(e)

joint signatory cosignataire *m/f*

joint venture joint-venture *f*, coentreprise *f*

journal *(accounts book)* journal *m*, livre-journal *m*

junior clerk employé(e) subalterne

junk bonds obligations *fpl* spéculatives non garanties

junk mail prospectus *mpl* publicitaires

jurisdiction juridiction *f*

K

keen competition compétition *f* acharnée, concurrence *f* vive

keen prices prix *mpl* compétitifs

keep a promise tenir une promesse

keep up with the demand satisfaire à la demande

key *(on keyboard)* touche *f*

key post poste *m* clé

kilo/kilogram kilo *m*, kilogramme *m*

knock down (v) (a price) baisser (un prix)

knock off *(reduce price)* baisser un prix de, faire un rabais de; *(stop work)* arrêter le travail, débrayer

L

label (n) étiquette *f*, label *m*

label (v) étiqueter

labour/labor costs coût *m* de la main-d'œuvre

labour/labor disputes conflits *mpl* du travail

lack of funds manque *m* de fonds

land (n) terre *f*, terrain *m*

land goods at a port débarquer des marchandises dans un port

landed costs prix *m* à quai

landing charges frais *mpl* de débarquement

landlord propriétaire *m*

lapse (v) expirer, n'être plus valide

late (adv) en retard

latest le dernier, la dernière, le plus récent, la plus récente

lawful trade commerce *m* licite

lawsuit procès *m*

lawyer avocat(e)

lay off workers mettre à pied/ licencier des ouvriers

lease (n) bail *m*, location-bail *f*

lease (v) *(of landlord)* louer à bail

lease equipment louer du matériel en crédit-bail

lease-back cession-bail *m*

leasing crédit-bail *m*, leasing *m*

ledger registre *m*, grand livre

legal *(referring to law)* légal(e), juridique

legal adviser conseiller *m* juridique

legal costs/charges frais *mpl* de justice

legal proceedings procès *m*, poursuites *fpl* judiciaires

legal status situation *f* légale, statut légal

lend prêter

lender prêteur *m*

lending limit plafond *m* de crédit

lessee locataire *m/f* à bail

lessor bailleur, bailleresse

letter of complaint lettre *f* de réclamation

letter of credit (L/C) lettre *f* de crédit

letter of reference lettre *f* de recommandation

level niveau *m*

level off/out se stabiliser

leverage ratio *m* d'endettement; effet *m* de levier

levy (n) impôt *m*, contribution *f*

levy (v) lever/percevoir (un impôt)

liabilities dettes *fpl*, passif *m*

liable for responsable de

liable to passible de

licence (n) autorisation *f*, permis *m*

license (v) autoriser, octroyer un permis

lien droit *m* de retention

life assurance assurance-vie *f*

lift (v) an embargo lever l'embargo

limit (n) limite *f*

limit (v) limiter

limited company (Ltd) société *f* à responsabilité limitée (S.A.R.L.)

limited liability
responsabilité *f* limitée
liquid assets
disponibilités *fpl*, liquidités *fpl*
liquidate a company
liquider une entreprise
liquidate stock liquider du stock
liquidation liquidation *f* d'un société
liquidator liquidateur *m*
liquidity liquidité *f*
list (n) *(catalogue/catalog)*
catalogue *m*
list price prix *m* catalogue
load (v) **(a computer program)**
charger (un programme)
load a truck/a ship charger un
camion/un navire
loan (n) prêt *m*; emprunt *m*
loan (v) prêter
loan capital capital *m* d'emprunt
local labour/labor
main-d'œuvre *f* locale
lock (n) serrure *f*
lock (v) fermer à clé
lock up a shop fermer un magasin (à
la fin de la journée)
lock up capital bloquer/immobiliser
des capitaux
logo logo *m*
long credit crédit *m* à long terme
long-dated bill
effet *m* à longue échéance
long-standing agreement accord *m*
de longue date
long-term loan prêt *m*/emprunt *m* à
long terme
long-term objectives objectifs *mpl* à
long terme
long-term planning planification *f*
à long terme
loose en vrac
lose (v) **an order**
perdre une commande
lose money perdre de l'argent
loss *(not a profit)* déficit *m*
loss *(of sth.)* perte *f*
loss-leader produit *m* d'appel,
article-réclame *m*
low sales ventes *fpl* médiocres
lower (v) **prices** baisser les prix
luggage bagages *mpl*
lump sum montant *m*/
paiement *m*/forfaitaire

M

magazine revue *f*,
magazine *m*, périodique *m*
magazine insert
encart *m* publicitaire
mail (n) courrier *m*;
(postal system) poste *f*
mail (v) poster, expédier, envoyer
par la poste
mail shot mailing *m*
mail-order vente *f* par
correspondance (VPC)
mail-order catalogue/catalog
catalogue *m* de vente par
correspondance
mailing list fichier *m* d'adresses
main office bureau *m* principal,
siège *m* social
maintain maintenir, entretenir
maintenance *(keeping in working
order)* entretien *m*, maintenance *f*
major shareholder
actionnaire *m* important
majority majorité *f*
majority shareholder
actionnaire *m* majoritaire
make good compenser, réparer
make money faire un gain/un profit
make out *(invoice)* rédiger, établir
make up for compenser
man (v) **(a stand, etc.)** assurer une
permanence (à un stand, etc.)
man-hour
heure/homme *f*, heure travaillée
manage property
gérer une propriété
manage to arriver à, réussir à
management *(action)* gestion *f*,
management *m*, direction *f*
management *(managers)*
la direction, l'administration *f*;
les cadres
management team équipe *f*
dirigeante, équipe de direction
manager *(of branch/shop)* directeur
(-trice) d'agence; gérant(e)
managerial staff personnel *m*
de direction
managing director (MD) directeur
(-trice) général(e)
manning levels besoins *mpl*
en effectifs

manpower main-d'œuvre f
manpower shortage pénurie f
de main-d'œuvre
manual (adj) manuel (-elle)
manual (n) manuel m, livret m
manual work travail m manuel
manual worker manœuvre m,
travailleur m manuel
manufacture (v) fabriquer,
manufacturer, usiner
manufactured goods articles mpl/
produits mpl manufacturés
manufacturer
fabricant m, constructeur m
manufacturing costs coûts mpl/
frais mpl de fabrication
margin (profit) marge f
marginal pricing méthode m de
coûts marginaux
maritime trade
commerce m maritime
mark (v) marquer, noter
mark down (an item) réduire le prix
(de), démarquer
mark up (an item) augmenter/
majorer le prix (de)
mark-up (profit margin)
marge f bénéficiaire
market (n) (possible sales)
marché m
market (v) vendre, commercialiser
market analysis analyse f du marché
market forces/trends tendances fpl
du marché
market leader
N° 1 du marché, leader m
market opportunities créneaux mpl
market penetration pénétration f
du marché
market research étude f
de marché
market share part f du marché
marketing marketing m,
commercialisation f
marketing department service m
du marketing
marketing manager directeur (-trice)
du marketing
marketing strategy stratégie f
commerciale
mass market product produit m
grand public

mass media médias mpl
mass production production f/
fabrication f en série
maternity leave
congé m de maternité
matter (n) (to be discussed)
point m, question f
matter (v)
avoir de l'importance, importer
maturity date date f d'échéance
maximum (adj) maximum,
maximal(e); (n) maximum m
MD (managing director) directeur
(-trice) général(e)
mean (n) moyenne f
mean annual increase augmentation
annuelle moyenne
means (money) moyens mpl
measurement of profitability
analyse f de la rentabilité, mesure f
du rendement
medium-sized moyen(ne)
medium-term à moyen terme
meet (so.) rencontrer (qqn); se
rencontrer, se réunir
meet a deadline respecter un délai
meet a demand satisfaire/répondre à
la demande
meet a target atteindre un objectif
meeting réunion f, assemblée f
memo note f, mémorandum m
merchandise (n) marchandise f
merchandize a product
commercialiser un produit
merchandizing marchandisage m,
merchandising m
merchant bank banque f d'affaires
merge fusionner
merger fusion f
message message m
middle management
cadres mpl moyens
middle-sized company entreprise f
de taille moyenne
middleman intermédiaire m
minimum (adj) minimum, minimal(e)
minimum (n) minimum m
minimum payment
paiement m minimum
minimum wage
salaire m minimum (garanti)

minority minorité *f*
minority shareholder
actionnaire *m* minoritaire
minus factor facteur *m* négatif
minutes *(meeting)* procès-verbal *m*
miscalculate
faire une erreur de calcul
miscalculation erreur *f* de calcul
miscellaneous divers(e), varié(e)
miss *(not to hit)* manquer, rater; *(not to meet)* manquer (qqn)
mistake erreur *f*, faute *f*
misunderstanding malentendu *m*
mixed economy économie *f* mixte
mobile phone téléphone *m* mobile
mobilize capital
mobiliser des capitaux
mock-up maquette *f*
model (n) modèle *m*
model agreement accord-type *m*
modem modem *m*
moderate (adj) modéré(e)
modes of payment
modalités *fpl* de paiement
monetary monétaire
money argent *m*
money order mandat *m* postal,
mandat-poste *m*
money supply masse *f* monétaire
money up front avance *f*, paiement
m d'avance
monitor (n) *(screen)* écran *m*
(d'ordinateur)
monitor (v) contrôler, vérifier
monopoly monopole *m*
month-end accounts comptes *mpl*
de fin de mois
monthly (adj) mensuel (-elle)
monthly payments paiements *mpl*
mensuels, mensualités *fpl*
monthly statement
relevé *m* mensuel
moratorium moratoire *m*
mortgage (n) hypothèque *f*,
prêt *m* hypothécaire
mortgage (v) prêter sur hypothèque
most-favored nation
nation *f* la plus favorisée
motivated motivé(e)
motivation motivation *f*
multilateral agreement
accord *m* multilatéral
multinational (n) multinationale *f*

multiple (adj) multiple
multiple entry visa visa permanent
(bon pour plusieurs entrées)
multiply multiplier

N

nationalized industry
industrie *f* nationalisée
nationwide
national(e), à l'échelon national
natural resources
ressources *fpl* naturelles
natural wastage
départs *mpl* naturels
negotiable négociable
negotiable instrument
effet *m* négociable
negotiate négocier
negotiation négociation *f*
negotiator négociateur (-trice)
net (adj) net, nette
net assets actif *m* net
net income/salary revenu *m* net,
salaire *m* net
net margin marge *f* nette
net price prix *m* net
net profit
bénéfice *m* net, gain *m* net
net weight poids *m* net
net yield rendement *m* net
network (v) *(computers)* connecter
en réseau
niche créneau *m*
nil return état *m* néant
no-claims bonus bonus *m*
no-strike agreement/clause clause *f*
interdisant la grève
nominal capital capital *m* nominal
nominal value valeur *f* nominale
nominee personne *f* désignée
non profit-making non lucratif (-ive),
sans but lucratif
non-negotiable instrument effet *m*
non-négociable
non-payment *(of a debt)*
non-paiement *m*
non-refundable deposit arrhes *fpl*
non remboursables
non-returnable packing emballage *m*
perdu/non consigné
note (n) avis *m*, note *f*
notice *(time allowed)* préavis *m*

notification notification f, avis m
notify notifier
null nul, nulle
number (n) *(figure)* numéro m
number (v) numéroter

O

objective (adj) objectif (-ive)
objective (n) objectif m
obligation *(duty)* obligation f
obsolescence obsolescence f
obsolete
    qui n'est plus en usage, périmé(e)
obtain obtenir, se procurer
obtainable
    qu'on peut se procurer, disponible
odd numbers nombres impairs
off *(away from work)* absent(e);
    (cancelled) annulé(e)
off-peak
    en dehors des heures de pointe
off-season morte-saison f
offer (n) offre f
offer (v) *(to buy)* offrir, proposer
office hours heures fpl de bureau
office staff personnel m de bureau
official (adj) officiel (-elle)
official (n) fonctionnaire m
offshore offshore
oil *(petroleum)* pétrole m
oil price prix m du pétrole
old-fashioned démodé(e)
on account en acompte
on approval à l'essai, à condition
on behalf of au nom de
on business pour affaires
on order
    commandé(e), en commande
on sale en vente
on time à l'heure
one-off isolé(e), unique
open (adj) *(not closed)* ouvert(e)
open (v) *(start new business)* ouvrir
open a bank account ouvrir un
    compte en banque
open a line of credit autoriser/ouvrir
    une ligne de crédit
open account compte ouvert
open credit découvert m autorisé,
    crédit m à découvert
open market marché m libre
open the meeting ouvrir la séance

open-plan office bureau m
    à modules, bureau paysager
opening balance bilan initial
opening hours heures fpl d'ouverture
opening stock stock m initial,
    stock d'ouverture
opening time heure f d'ouverture
operate être en vigueur
operating costs coûts opérationnels,
    coûts d'exploitation
operating manual
    manuel m d'utilisation
operating profit
    bénéfice m commercial
operational costs
    coûts mpl opérationnels
operator opérateur (-trice)
    (d'une machine)
option to purchase option f d'achat
optional extras accessoires mpl
    facultatifs/en option
order (n) *(for goods)* commande f;
    (instruction) ordre m;
    (money) mandat m
order (v) *(goods)* commander
order fulfilment exécution f
    de commandes
order number
    numéro m de commande
order processing traitement m
    de commandes
order, on commandé, en commande
ordinary shares
    actions fpl ordinaires
organization chart organigramme m
organize organiser
origin, country of pays m d'origine
original (adj) original(e), d'origine
out of date démodé(e), dépassé(e)
out of stock *(article)* épuisé(e);
    (supplier) en rupture de stock
out of work au/en chômage
outgoing mail courrier m au départ
outgoings sorties fpl, dépenses fpl
outlay dépense f
output (n) *(goods)*
    production f, rendement m
outside office hours en dehors des
    heures de bureau
outsize (OS) grande taille f
outstanding exceptionnel (-elle);
    (unpaid) à payer; impayé(e)

outstanding debts créances *fpl*, dettes *fpl* à payer; impayés *mpl*

outstanding orders commandes *fpl* en attente

overbook surréserver, faire un surbooking

overbooking surréservation *f*, surbooking *m*

overcapacity surcapacité *f*

overcharge (n) trop-perçu *m*

overcharge (v) faire payer trop cher

overdraft découvert *m*

overdrawn account compte *m* à découvert

overdue en retard

overheads frais *mpl* généraux, frais d'administration générale

overproduction surproduction *f*

overseas markets marchés *mpl* étrangers

overseas trade commerce *m* extérieur

overspend one's budget dépasser son budget

overstocks excédents *m* de stock

overtime heures *f* supplémentaires

overtime pay (tarif des) heures supplémentaires

owe devoir

owing to en raison de, à cause de

own label/own brand goods produits à marque du distributeur

owner propriétaire *m/f*

ownership propriété *f*

P

pack (n) paquet *m*

pack (v) emballer, empaqueter

package deal contrat *m* global; forfait *m*

packaging material emballage *m*, conditionnement *m*

packing list/slip liste *f* de colisage

paid *(invoice)* payé(e), réglé(e)

pallet palette *f*

palletize mettre sur palettes

paper bag sac *m*/pochette *f* en paier

paper loss perte *f* théorique

paper profit bénéfice *m* théorique, gain *m* théorique

paperwork paperasserie *f*

par value valeur *f* nominale, valeur au pair

parcel (n) paquet *m*, colis *m*

parcel post service *m* colis (postaux)

parent company maison *f* mère, société *f* mère

part exchange reprise *f* (contre un achat)

part-time work/employment travail *m* à temps partiel/à mi-temps

partial payment acompte *m*

particulars détails *mpl*, coordonnées *fpl*, description *f*

partner associé(e)

party *(to contract, etc.)* partie *f*

patent brevet *m*

patent pending/applied for demande de brevet déposée

pay (n) *(salary)* salaire *m*, paie *f*, traitement *m*, rémunération *f*

pay a bill régler/payer une note

pay an invoice régler une facture

pay back rembourser

pay by cheque/check régler/payer par chèque

pay by credit card payer avec une carte de crédit

pay cash payer comptant

pay cheque/check chèque *m* de salaire

pay in advance payer d'avance

pay out verser de l'argent

pay rise augmentation *f* de salaire

payable in advance payable à l'avance

payable on demand payable à vue/sur présentation

payee bénéficiaire *m/f*

payer payeur *m*

paying-in slip bordereau *m* de versement

payment paiement *m*, règlement *m*, versement *m*

payment in cash paiement *m* en espèces/au comptant/en cash

payment on account acompte *m*

peak period heures *fpl* de pointe

peg (v) *prices* bloquer les prix

penalize pénaliser, sanctionner

penalty clause clause *f* pénale

pending en attente

penetrate a market pénétrer un marché, s'implanter sur un marché

pension pension *f* de retraite
per annum par année
per day par jour
per hour à/de l'heure
percentage pourcentage *m*; taux *m*
percentage discount pourcentage *m* de remise
period période *f*, durée *f*
perishable goods denrées *fpl* périssables
permission permission *f*, autorisation *f*
permit (n) permis *m*
permit (v) autoriser qqn à faire qch.
personal assistant (PA) secrétaire/ assistant(e) de direction
personal computer (PC) ordinateur *m* personnel
personnel personnel *m*
personnel manager chef *m* du personnel
petty cash petite caisse *f*
petty expenses petites/menues dépenses *fpl*
phase in introduire graduellement
phase out mettre fin graduellement
phone (n) téléphone *m*
phone (v) téléphoner
phone call appel *m* (téléphonique)
phone card télécarte *f*
phone number numéro *m* de téléphone
photocopier photocopieur *m*
photocopy (n) photocopie *f*
photocopy (v) photocopier
pie chart diagramme *m* circulaire
piece rate tarif *m* unitaire
piecework travail *m* à la pièce/ aux pièces
pilferage, pilfering chapardage *m*
pilot scheme programme *m* pilote
place (n) **of work** lieu *m* de travail
place (v) **an order** passer une commande
plaintiff partie *f* plaignante
plan (n) (drawing) plan *m*; (project) plan *m*, projet *m*
plan (v) planifier; projeter
plane avion *m*
plant (n) (machinery) machines *fpl*
plug (v) (publicize) faire de la publicité
plus factor atout *m*

point of sale point *m* de vente
policy politique *f*
poor quality qualité *f* inférieure
poor service service *m* médiocre
popular prices prix *mpl* à la portée de tous
port (computer; harbour/harbor) port *m*
port of call port *m* d'escale
port of embarkation port *m* d'embarquement
portable portatif (-ive), portable
portfolio portefeuille *f* (d'actions)
POS material (point of sale material) matériel *m* de publicité sur le lieu de vente (PLV)
position (job) poste *m*
positive positif (-ive)
possess posséder
post (n) (job) poste *m*, emploi *m*; (letters) courrier *m*
post (v) poster, mettre à la poste
post free franco de port, franc de port
postage tarif *m* postal
postage and packing (p & p) frais *mpl* de port et d'emballage
postage paid port payé
postal charges/rates tarifs *mpl* postaux
postcode code *m* postal
postpaid port payé
postpone remettre à plus tard, reporter
postponement renvoi *m*, remise *f* à plus tard
potential market marché *m* potentiel
pound (money) livre *f* (sterling); (weight, 0.45kg) livre *f*
power of attorney procuration *f*
preference shares actions *fpl* privilégiées
premises locaux *mpl*
premium (insurance) prime *f* d'assurance
premium offer prime *f*, cadeau *m*
prepack(age) préemballer, conditionner
prepaid payé d'avance
prepayment paiement *m* d'avance

present

present (adj) *(being there)*
présent(e); *(now)* actuel (-elle)

present (v) *(show a document)*
présenter

present a bill for acceptance
présenter une traite à l'acceptation

presentation *(exhibition; showing a
document)* présentation f

press conference conférence f
de presse

press release communiqué m
de presse

pretax profit
bénéfice m avant impôts

price (n) prix m

price (v) fixer/déterminer un prix

price ceiling plafond m des prix

price controls contrôle m des prix

price ex warehouse prix m départ
entrepôt, prix ex-entrepôt

price ex works prix m départ usine

price label/tag étiquette f de prix

price list catalogue m, tarif m, liste f
de prix

price war guerre f des prix

price/earnings ratio coefficient m
de capitalisation des résultats,
PER m

pricing policy politique f (de fixation)
des prix

primary industry industrie f de base,
secteur m primaire

prime cost prix m de revient de base

principal (adj) principal(e)

principle principe m

print out imprimer

printer *(machine)* imprimante f

printout sortie f d'imprimante

private enterprise
entreprise f privée

private property propriété f privée

private sector secteur m privé

privatization privatisation f

privatize privatiser

pro forma facture f pro forma

pro rata au prorata

problem area secteur m difficile

process (v) *(deal with)*
traiter, exécuter

processing of information
traitement m de données

product produit m

product design conception f
de produit

product line gamme f/ligne f
de produits

product mix éventail m/
gamme f de produits

production *(making)*
fabrication f, production f

production department service m de
la production/de la fabrication

production manager
chef m de la fabrication

production targets objectifs mpl
de production

productive discussions
discussions fpl productives

productivity
productivité f, rendement m

productivity agreement contrat m
de productivité

professional (n) *(expert)*
spécialiste m, expert m

professional qualifications
qualifications fpl professionnelles

profit profit m, bénéfice m, gain m

profit and loss account compte m de
pertes et profits

profit before/after tax bénéfice m
avant/après impôts

profit centre/center centre m
de profit

profit margin marge f bénéficiaire

profitability rentabilité f

profitable rentable

program a computer
programmer un ordinateur

programme/program
programme m, logiciel m

progress chaser responsable m/f
de suivi

progress report rapport m
d'avancement du travail

project *(plan)* projet m, plan m

project manager chef m de projet

projected sales ventes fpl prévues

promissory note billet m à ordre

promote *(advertise)* faire de la
publicité; *(give better job)* donner
de l'avancement, promouvoir

promote a new product lancer un
nouveau produit

promotion *(publicity; to better job)*
promotion f

promotional budget
budget *m* promotionnel
prompt payment
paiement *m* immédiat
prompt service service *m* rapide
proportion part *f*, partie *f*
proportional proportionnel (-elle)
propose to (*do sth.*) proposer de
proprietor (-tress) propriétaire *m/f*
prosecution (*legal action*)
poursuites *fpl* judiciaires
prospect client *m* potentiel
prospective buyer acheteur *m*
potentiel, prospect *m*
prospects perspectives *fpl* (d'avenir)
prospectus prospectus *m*
protest strike grève *f* de protestation
provided that/providing à condition
(que/de), pourvu que
provision (*condition*)
stipulation *f*, clause *f*
provisional budget
budget *m* provisoire
proviso condition *f*
proxy vote vote *m* par procuration
public finance finances *fpl* publiques
public holiday jour *m* férié
Public Limited Company (Plc)
société *f* anonyme (S.A.)
public relations (PR)
relations *fpl* publiques
public relations department
service *m* des relations publiques
public sector secteur *m* public
public transport
transports *mpl* en commun
publicity publicité *f*
publicity budget
budget *m* publicitaire
publicity department service *m*
de publicité
publicity manager directeur (-trice)
de la publicité
publicize faire de la publicité pour
purchase (n) achat *m*, acquisition *f*
purchase (v) acheter, acquérir
purchase tax taxe *f* à l'achat
purchaser acheteur *m*, acquéreur *m*
purchasing achat *m*
purchasing power pouvoir *m* d'achat
put in writing
mettre par écrit, rédiger

Q

qualified (*skilled*) qualifié(e)
qualify as se spécialiser, faire des
études spécialisées
quality control contrôle *m* de qualité
quantity quantité *f*
quantity discount
remise *f* sur quantité
quarter (*25%*) quart *m*
quarter (*three months*) trimestre *m*
quarterly (adj) trimestriel (-elle)
quay quai *m*
quota quota *m*, contingent *m*
quotation, quote (*estimate*) devis *m*
quote (v) (*estimate*) donner un prix

R

rail chemin *m* de fer
railway chemin *m* de fer
railway station gare *f*
(de chemin de fer)
raise (v) (*increase*) augmenter;
(*obtain money*) se procurer des
fonds, trouver des capitaux
raise an invoice rédiger une facture
random check contrôle *m* aléatoire
random error erreur *f* aléatoire
random sample
échantillon *m* aléatoire
rate (n) (*amount*) taux *m*;
(*price*) tarif *m*, prix *m*
rate of exchange taux *m* de change
rate of inflation taux *m* d'inflation
rating (*credit*) notation *f*, note *f*
financière (d'une société)
ratio ratio *m*, taux *m*, rapport *m*
rationalize rationaliser
raw materials matières *fpl* premières
reach a decision
prendre une décision
reach an agreement
arriver à un accord
ready prêt(e)
ready cash argent *m* comptant/cash
real estate biens *mpl* immobiliers
real income/wages revenu *m* net,
salaire *m* net
realizable assets actif *m* réalisable
realize property/assets réaliser une
propriété/des biens
reappoint désigner de, à nouveau

reassess

reassess réévaluer
rebate remboursement m
receipt *(paper)* reçu m, quittance f;
  (receiving) réception f
receipts recettes fpl
receivables
  comptes mpl clients, créances fpl
receive recevoir, réceptionner
  (des marchandises)
receiver *(liquidator)*
  administrateur m judiciaire
reception réception f
reception desk bureau m de la
  réception; bureau d'accueil
receptionist réceptionniste m/f
recession récession f
reciprocal trade
  commerce m bilatéral
recommend *(say sth. is good)*
  recommander (un produit, etc.)
recommend *(suggest)* recommander/
  conseiller (de faire qch.)
reconcile faire concorder (deux
  comptes/deux états)
reconciliation
  réconciliation f, rapprochement m
record (v)
  noter, consigner, enregistrer
record sales/losses/profits
  ventes/pertes/profits record
records archives fpl, dossiers mpl
recover *(get better)* se remettre,
  se reprendre
recover *(get sth. back)* récupérer,
  recouvrer, retrouver
recovery *(getting better)* reprise f/
  relance f (de l'économie)
recovery *(getting sth. back)*
  recouvrement m, récupération f
red tape
  paperasserie f administrative
redeem rembourser, amortir
redemption (of a debt)
  remboursement m (d'une dette)
redemption date date f d'échéance
  du remboursement
reduce réduire, diminuer
reduce a price baisser un prix
reduced rate tarif m réduit
redundancy licenciement m
redundant *(personnel)* licencié
refer *(to item)* se reporter à, se
  référer à; mentionner

reference *(person)* répondant m;
  (report) référence f,
  recommandation f
reference number
  numéro m de référence f
refund (n) remboursement m
refund (v) rembourser
refundable deposit
  avance f remboursable
refusal refus m
refuse (v) refuser
regarding concernant
regardless of malgré, sans
  considération de
register (n) *(official list)* registre m,
  état m, liste f
register (v) *(in official list)* enregistrer,
  inscrire, immatriculer
register (v) *(a letter)* recommander
  (une lettre)
register a company
  immatriculer une société
registered design modèle déposé
registered office siège m social
registered trademark
  marque f déposée
registration enregistrement m
registration fee droit m
  d'enregistrement/d'inscription
registry bureau m d'état civil; bureau
  d'enregistrement
regular *(always at same time)*
  régulier (-ière), habituel (-elle)
regular *(ordinary)*
  ordinaire, normal(e)
regular customer client fidèle
regulate *(by law)* réglementer
regulations règlements mpl
reinvest réinvestir
reinvestment réinvestissement m
reject (n) article imparfait/de rebut
reject (v) rejeter, refuser
relating to se rapportant à, relatif à,
  en rapport avec
relations relations fpl
release (v) *(make public)* publier
release dues liquider les commandes
  en attente
reliability fiabilité f
reliable honnête, fiable, sûr(e)
remain *(be left)* rester
remainder *(things left)*
  reste m, reliquat m

remit by cheque/check régler
par chèque
remittance règlement m
remunerate rémunérer, rétribuer
remuneration rémunération f
render an account (to invoice)
présenter un compte, facturer
renew a bill of exchange prolonger
une traite
renew a lease renouveler un bail
renewal of a bill prolongation f
d'une traite
renewal of a lease renouvellement m
d'un bail
rent (n) loyer m
rent (v) (pay money for) louer
rental loyer m, prix m de location
reorder (n) commande de
réapprovisionnement
reorder (v) renouveler une
commande, se réapprovisionner
reorder level
niveau m de réapprovisionnement
reorganization réorganisation f
reorganize réorganiser
repay rembourser
repayable remboursable
repeat an order
renouveler une commande
repeat order
nouvelle commande f, commande
de réapprovisionnement
replacement (item) remplacement m
replacement value
valeur f de remplacement
reply (n) réponse f; (v) répondre
report (n) rapport m
report (v) signaler; faire un rapport
report (v) **to so.** relever (directement)
de qqn
represent représenter;
faire de la représentation
representative (person)
représentant(e), délégué(e)
commercial(e), VRP m/f
request (n) demande f, requête f
request (v) demander, solliciter
request, on sur demande
requirements besoins mpl
resale revente f
research and development (R & D)
Recherche et développement
researcher chercheur (-euse)

reservation réservation f
reserve (n) (money) réserve f
reserve (supplies)
réserves fpl, provisions fpl
residence permit permis m de séjour
resident (adj) résident(e)
resign démissionner
resources ressources fpl
response réaction f
responsibility responsabilité f
responsible (for) responsable (de)
responsible to so. relever de qqn
restock se réapprovisionner
restrict limiter
restrictive practices
pratiques fpl restrictives
restructure restructurer
restructuring of a loan
restructuration f d'un emprunt
result from découler de, provenir de
result in avoir pour résultat de
results (profit or loss) résultats mpl
resume negotiations
reprendre les négociations
retail (v) (goods) vendre des
marchandises au détail
retail (v) (sell for a price) se vendre à
retail price prix m de détail
retail price index indice m des prix à
la consommation
retailer détaillant(e)
retire (from one's job) prendre sa
retraite, partir à la retraite
retirement age âge m de la retraite
retrain recycler qqn, se recycler
retrenchment compression f
des dépenses
return (n) (declaration) déclaration f;
(profit) revenu m, rendement m
return (n) (sending back) retour m
return address adresse f
de l'expéditeur
return on investment (ROI)
rentabilité f d'un investissement
returns (unsold goods)
invendus mpl, retours mpl
revenue recette f, rentrée f, revenu m
revoke révoquer, annuler
revolving credit crédit m
permanent/renouvelable
right (n) (legal title) droit m
right of way (on land) servitude f

rightful owner

rightful owner
propriétaire m/f légitime
rights issue émission f prioritaire
rise (n) (increase) augmentation f;
(salary) augmentation f (de salaire)
rise (v) augmenter
risk (n) risque m
risk (v) (money) risquer
risk capital capital-risque m
risky risqué(e), hasardeux (-euse)
rival company société f concurrente
road transport
transports mpl routiers
rock-bottom prices
prix mpl les plus bas
roll over credit/a debt reconduire un
crédit/une dette
room (space) place f
rough calculation
calcul m approximatif
rough estimate
estimation f approximative
round down/up arrondir au chiffre
inférieur/supérieur
routine work travail m
habituel/routinier
royalty royalties fpl, redevances fpl
rule (v) (give decision)
déclarer, statuer
ruling (n) décision f, jugement m
run (v) (manage) diriger, gérer
run into debt s'endetter
run out of (stock) manquer de
running costs/expenses coûts mpl
opérationnels, coûts d'exploitation
running total total m reporté
rush hour heures fpl de pointe
rush order commande f urgente

S

sack so. renvoyer/licencier qqn
safe (n) coffre-fort m
safe investment placement m sûr
safeguard sauvegarder, protéger
safety precautions
mesures fpl de sécurité
safety regulations
consignes fpl de sécurité
salaried salarié(e)
salary salaire m
salary review révision f de salaire

sale (n) (at a low price) solde m;
(selling) vente f
sales ventes fpl
sales budget budget m commercial,
budget des ventes
sales campaign campagne f de
vente(s), campagne commerciale
sales conference
réunion f du service commercial
sales department
service m commercial
sales figures chiffre m des ventes,
chiffre d'affaires
sales forecast
prévisions fpl des ventes
sales manager chef m des ventes,
directeur (-trice) commercial(e)
sales target objectif m de vente
sales tax taxe f sur les ventes
salesman (in shop) vendeur m
salesman (representative)
représentant(e), délégué(e)
commercial(e), VRP m/f
salvage (n) (action) sauvetage m
salvage (v)
sauver, effectuer un sauvetage
sample (n) échantillon m
satisfy (customer) satisfaire
satisfy a demand satisfaire/répondre
à la demande
saturate the market
saturer le marché
save (v) (money) économiser, faire
des économies; (data)
sauvegarder
savings account
compte m d'épargne
scale down/scale up réduire/
augmenter suivant un barème
scale of charges tarif m, barème m
des prix
scheduled flight vol m régulier
sealed tenders
soumissions fpl cachetées
season (time of year) saison f
season ticket carte f d'abonnement
seasonal demand
demande saisonnière
seasonal variations
variations fpl saisonnières
secondary industry industrie f
de transformation, secteur m
secondaire

secondhand d'occasion

seconds articles *mpl* déclassés/de second choix

secretary secrétaire *m/f*

sector secteur *m*

secure (v) **funds** se procurer des fonds

secured creditor créancier privilégié

secured loan emprunt *m* garanti

securities titres *mpl*, valeurs *fpl*

security guard vigile *m*, gardien *m* de la sécurité

security of employment sécurité *f* de l'emploi

seize saisir, confisquer

seizure saisie *f*, confiscation *f*

self-employed qui travaille à son compte, indépendant(e)

self-financing (adj) qui peut s'autofinancer

sell vendre

sell forward vendre à terme

sell-by date date *f* limite de vente

selling (n) vente *f*

semi-skilled workers ouvriers *mpl* spécialisés

send an invoice by post envoyer une facture par la poste

sender expéditeur (-trice)

senior manager/executive cadre *m* supérieur

separate (adj) séparé(e)

separate cover, under sous pli séparé

serial number numéro *m* de série

serve a customer servir un client

service (n) *(dealing with customers)* service *m*; *(of machine)* entretien *m*, maintenance *f*

service (v) *(a machine)* réviser une machine

service charge service *m*

service department service *m* d'entretien

service industry industrie *f* de services

service manual manuel *m* d'entretien

set (adj) fixé(e)

set price prix *m* imposé, prix fixe

set up a company créer/constituer/ fonder une société

setback revers *m*, recul *m*

settle (an invoice) payer/régler (une facture)

settle an account solder/régler un compte

settlement *(payment)* règlement *m*, paiement *m*

share (n) *(in a company)* action *f*

share (v) *(divide among)* partager

share/stock certificate certificat *m* d'action *f*

shareholder actionnaire *m/f*

shareholding actions *f*; participation *f*

shelf life of a product durée *f* de conservation d'un produit

shelve (v) repousser, ajourner; abandonner (un projet)

shelving *(postponing)* ajournement *m*

shelving *(shelves)* rayonnage *m*

shift (n) *(team of workers)* équipe *f*

shift work travail *m* posté, travail par équipe

ship (n) navire *m*

ship (v) expédier, envoyer

shipment *(sending)* expédition *f*, envoi *m*; *(load)* chargement *m*

shipper expéditeur *m*

shipping charges/costs frais *mpl* de transport

shipping instructions instructions *fpl* pour l'expédition

shop around comparer les prix (dans différents magasins)

shopper acheteur (-euse), client(e)

shopping centre/center centre *m* commercial

short credit crédit *m* à court terme

short of à court de, pas assez de

short-term (adj) à court terme

short-term loan emprunt *m* à court terme; prêt *m* à court terme

shortage manque *m*, pénurie *f*

shortlist (n) liste *f* de sélection

shortlist (v) sélectionner (des candidats)

show a profit produire un bénéfice

sideline activité *f* secondaire

sight draft traite *f* à vue

sign (n) panneau *m* publicitaire, enseigne *f*

sign (v) signer

signatory signataire *m/f*

signature signature *f*

simple interest intérêts *mpl* simples

sister company société-sœur *f*

site site *m*, emplacement *m*

site engineer
ingénieur *m* de chantier

situation *(state of affairs)*
situation *f*, état *m*

situations vacant offres *fpl* d'emploi;
postes à pourvoir

skeleton staff personnel *m* réduit,
personnel de base

skill aptitude *f*, talent *m*; technique *f*

skilled workers
ouvriers *mpl* qualifiés

slack peu actif (-ive)

slash prices casser les prix

sleeping partner commanditaire *m*

slip *(piece of paper)* fiche *f*,
bordereau *m*; *(mistake)* erreur *f*

slow payer mauvais payeur

slump in sales
effondrement *m* des ventes

small businesses petites et
moyennes entreprises (PME)

small-scale peu important(e),
modeste

social costs coûts *mpl* sociaux

social security sécurité *f* sociale

socio-economic groups groupes *mpl*
socio-économiques

soft currency devise *f* faible

software programme *m*, logiciel *m*

sole seul(e), exclusif (-ive)

sole agent agent *m* exclusif,
concessionnaire exclusif

sole owner seul propriétaire *m*

solicit orders
solliciter des commandes

solution solution *f*

solve a problem
résoudre un problème

solvency solvabilité *f*

solvent (adj) solvable

source of income source *f*
de revenus

spare part pièce *f* de rechange,
pièce détachée

special offer
offre *f* spéciale, promotion *f*

specification spécifications *fpl*,
cahier *m* des charges

specify spécifier, indiquer

spend *(money)* dépenser

spend time consacrer du temps à,
passer du temps à

spinoff produit *m* dérivé

sponsor (n) sponsor *m*, parrain *m*

sponsor (v) sponsoriser, parrainer

sponsorship
parrainage *m*, sponsorisation *f*

spread a risk répartir un risque

stability stabilité *f*

stabilize stabiliser, se stabiliser

stable currency monnaie *f* stable

staff meeting réunion *f* du personnel

staged payments
paiements *mpl* échelonnés

stagger étaler, échelonner

stamp (v) *(letter)* affranchir

stand (n) *(at exhibition)* stand *m*

standard (adj) ordinaire, standard

standard (n) norme *f*, standard *m*

standard rate *(of tax)* taux *m*
d'imposition de base

standardize standardiser,
normaliser

standby ticket
billet *m* (d'avion) stand-by

standing standing *m*, réputation *f*

staple industry industrie *f*
principale/de base

start-up costs frais *mpl* de
démarrage/d'établissement

starting salary salaire *m* de
départ/de débutant

state (n) *(condition)* état *m*

state-of-the-art de pointe

statement of account
relevé *m* de compte

statistical analysis
analyse *f* statistique

statistics statistiques *fpl*, chiffres *mpl*

status statut *m*, position *f*

status inquiry enquête *f* sur la
solvabilité d'un client

statute of limitations
loi *f* de prescription

statutory holiday congé *m* légal,
fête *f* légale

sterling livre *f* sterling

stipulate stipuler

stock (n) *(goods)* stock *m*

stock (v) *(goods)* stocker, entreposer

stock control contrôle *m*/gestion *f*
des stocks

Stock Exchange Bourse *f*
stock list inventaire *m*
stock market marché *m*, Bourse *f*
stock size taille *f* courante
stock up faire des réserves/
des provisions
stockbroker agent *m* de change
stockist stockiste *m/f*, dépositaire *m/f*
stocktaking inventaire *m* (des stocks)
stocktaking sale
soldes *mpl* avant inventaire
stop (v) *(doing sth.)* arrêter,
suspendre, cesser
stop a cheque/check faire opposition
à un chèque
stop payments
suspendre les paiements
storage (n) *(computer)* mémoire *f*
storage (n) *(cost)* frais *mpl*
d'entrepôt; *(in warehouse)*
entreposage
storage capacity
capacité *f* d'entreposage
storage facilities entrepôt *m*
store (n) *(large shop)* magasin *m*;
(grand) magasin; *(storage
place)* dépôt *m*, entrepôt *m*
store (v) *(keep in warehouse)*
entreposer
straight line depreciation
amortissement *m* linéaire
strategic planning stratégie *f*
strategy stratégie *f*
strike (n) grève *f*
strike (v) faire (la) grève, se mettre
en grève
striker gréviste *m/f*
strong currency devise *f* forte
subcontract (n)
contrat *m* de sous-traitance
subcontract (v) donner en sous-
traitance, sous-traiter
subcontractor sous-traitant *m*
subject to sous réserve de
sublease (n) sous-location *f*
sublease (v) sous-louer
subsidiary (adj) secondaire
subsidiary (n) filiale *f*
subsidize subventionner
subsidy subvention *f*
subtotal sous-total *m*
succeed *(do well)* réussir
success succès *m*

successful qui réussit,
qui a du succès
sue intenter un procès à/contre qqn;
poursuivre qqn (en justice)
sum *(of money)* somme *f*
sundries articles *mpl* divers
supervise superviser, surveiller
supervision surveillance *f*
supervisor surveillant(e)
supplementary supplémentaire
supplier fournisseur *m*
supply (n) *(action)* fourniture *f*
supply (v) approvisionner, fournir
supply price prix *m* livré
surcharge supplément *m*; surtaxe *f*
surplus surplus *m*, excédent *m*
surplus dividend superdividende *m*
surrender (n) *(insurance)* résiliation *f*
d'une police d'assurance
survey (n) *(building)* expertise *f*
survey (v) *(building)* expertiser
surveyor expert *m* (en bâtiments)
suspend suspendre
suspension of payments arrêt *m*/
suspension *f* des paiements
swap (n) échange *m*
swap (v) échanger
switch over to passer à
switchboard
standard *m* (téléphonique)
synergy synergie *f*
system système *m*
systems analyst informaticien-
analyste *m*, analyste *m* de
systèmes

T

tacit agreement accord *m* tacite
take a call répondre au téléphone,
prendre un appel
take action agir, intervenir, prendre
des mesures
take legal advice consulter un avocat
take off *(deduct)* enlever, déduire,
rabattre; *(plane)* décoller
take on more staff embaucher du
personnel supplémentaire
take out a policy souscrire/contracter
une assurance
take over *(from so. else)* prendre la
suite, prendre la succession
take place avoir lieu, arriver

take so. to court poursuivre qqn
en justice
take stock
faire l'inventaire des stocks
take the initiative prendre l'initiative
takeover
rachat *m*, prise *f* de contrôle
takeover bid offre *f* publique d'achat
(OPA)
takings recettes *fpl*
tangible assets biens *mpl* matériels,
actifs *mpl* corporels
target (n) objectif *m*, cible *f*
target (v) cibler
target market marché ciblé
tariff *(price)* tarif *m*
tariff barriers
barrières *fpl* douanières
tax (n) impôt *m*; taxe *f*
tax (v) imposer; taxer
tax allowance abattement *m* fiscal
tax assessment détermination *f* de
l'assiette fiscale
tax consultant conseiller *m* fiscal
tax deducted at source impôt *m*
retenu à la source
tax exemption exonération *f*/
exemption *f* d'impôt
tax rate taux *m* d'imposition
tax return/declaration déclaration *f*
de revenus
tax year année *f* fiscale
tax-deductible
déductible (des impôts)
tax-free hors taxe
taxable income revenu *m* imposable
taxpayer contribuable *m/f*
telephone (n) téléphone *m*
telephone (v) téléphoner, appeler
(au téléphone)
telephone directory
annuaire *m* des téléphones
telephone number
numéro *m* de téléphone
telephonist standardiste *m/f*
temp *(money)* secrétaire *f* intérimaire
temporary staff
personnel *m* temporaire
tenancy *(agreement)*
bail *m* de location
tenant locataire *m/f*
tender (n) soumission *f*
term *(validity)* terme *m*, durée *f*

term loan prêt *m* à terme
terminate an agreement
résilier un contrat
termination clause
clause *f* de résiliation
terms conditions *fpl*, termes *mpl*
terms of employment
conditions *fpl* d'emploi
terms of sale conditions *fpl* de vente
territory *(of salesman)* secteur *m*
tertiary industry
industrie *f* de services
test (n) test *m*, contrôle *m*
test (v) tester, contrôler
theft vol *m*
third party tiers *m*; tierce personne *f*
threshold price prix *m* de seuil
throughput rendement *m*
tie-up *(link)* association *f*
tighten up on resserrer (le contrôle)
time scale délai *m* (d'exécution)
time, on à l'heure; à temps
timetable (n) *(appointments)*
emploi *m* du temps, calendrier *m*
timetable (v) établir un calendrier
tip (n) *(money)* pourboire *m*
token charge
participation *f* symbolique
toll péage *m*
toll free gratuitement
ton tonne *f*
tonnage *(of ship)* tonnage *m*, jauge *f*
top management direction *f*
générale, cadres *mpl* supérieurs
top quality qualité *f* supérieure/extra
total (n) total *m*
total (v) s'élever à
total amount
total *m*, montant *m* total
total cost coût *m* total
total invoice value montant *m* total
de la facture
track record expérience *f*
professionnelle
trade (n) *(business)* commerce *m*
trade (v)
faire des opérations commerciales
trade directory
répertoire *m* des entreprises
trade discount
remise *f* commerciale, remise
professionnelle
trade fair foire *f* commerciale

trade in (v) donner en reprise
trade journal journal *m* professionnel
trade price prix *m* de gros
trade terms remise *f* professionnelle
trade union
syndicat *m*, Trade-union *f*
trade-in price valeur *f* de reprise
trademark, trade name marque *f*
de fabrique/de commerce
trader commerçant(e),
négociant(e), marchand(e)
trading loss perte *f* d'exploitation
trading partner
partenaire *m* commercial
trading profit
bénéfice *m* d'exploitation
train (v) *(learn)* suivre une formation;
(teach) former qqn
trainee stagiaire *m/f*; apprenti(e)
transact business traiter une affaire,
effectuer une transaction
transaction transaction *f*
transfer (n) transfert *m*
transfer of funds
virement *m* de crédit
transit transit *m*
transit visa visa *m* de transit
translation traduction *f*
transport (n) transport *m*
transport (v) transporter
trial balance bilan *m* de vérification
trial sample échantillon *m* d'essai
triplicate, in en trois exemplaires
true copy copie *f* conforme
turn down refuser
turn over (v) *(make sales)* faire un
chiffre d'affaires (de)
turnkey operation
opération *f* clés en main
turnover *(sales)* chiffre *m* d'affaires

U

unauthorized expenditure
dépenses *f* non autorisées
unavailable non disponible
unclaimed baggage bagages *mpl*
non réclamés
unconditional inconditionnel (-elle),
sans réserve
undated non daté(e)
under *(according to)* selon, aux
termes de

under *(less than)*
moins de, inférieur(e) à
under contract lié par contrat
under new management
changement *m* de propriétaire/
de direction
undercut a rival vendre moins cher
qu'un concurrent
undersell vendre moins cher que
undersigned soussigné(e)
understanding entente *f*;
arrangement *m*
undertaking *(company)* entreprise *f*;
(promise) engagement *m*
underwrite *(guarantee)* garantir
unemployed
sans emploi, au chômage
unemployment chômage *m*
unfair competition
concurrence *f* déloyale
**unfavourable/unfavorable exchange
rate** taux *m* de change
défavorable
unfulfilled order commande *f*
non exécutée
union syndicat *m*
unique selling point (USP) avantage *m* spécifique d'un produit
unique selling proposition (USP)
offre *f* unique
unit cost coût *m* unitaire
unit price prix *m* unitaire,
prix de l'unité
unload *(goods)* décharger
unobtainable
qu'on ne peut se procurer
unpaid invoices factures *fpl*
impayées, les impayés *mpl*
unsecured creditor
créancier *m* sans garantie
unsuccessful
qui ne réussit pas, sans succès
up front à l'avance, d'avance
up to date *(complete)* à jour;
(modern) moderne, de pointe
up-market
de luxe, (de) haut de gamme
update (v) mettre à jour, réviser
urgent urgent(e)
use (n) emploi *m*, utilisation *f*
use (v) utiliser, se servir de
user-friendly convivial(e)
utilization utilisation *f*

V

vacancy *(for job)* poste *m* vacant, poste à pourvoir
valid valide, valable
valuation évaluation *f*, expertise *f*
value (n) valeur *f*
value (v) évaluer, estimer
value added tax (VAT) taxe *f* sur la valeur ajoutée (TVA)
variable costs coûts *mpl* variables
VAT invoice facture *f* avec TVA
vendor vendeur *m*
venture capital capital-risque *m*
verbal agreement entente *f* verbale, accord *m* verbal
verification vérification *f*
verify vérifier
vested interest droits *mpl* acquis, intérêts *mpl*
veto a decision s'opposer à une décision, mettre son veto à une décision
visible trade commerce *m* visible
void (adj) *(not valid)* nul, nulle
void (v) annuler
volume discount ristourne *f*/remise *f* sur quantité
volume of trade/business volume *m* d'affaires
voluntary liquidation liquidation *f* volontaire
vote of thanks remerciements *mpl*
voucher bon *m* (d'échange)

W

wage paie *f*, salaire *m*
wage negotiations négociations *f* salariales
waive renoncer à
waiver clause clause *f* d'abandon
warehouse (n) entrepôt *m*
warehouse (v) entreposer
warehousing entreposage *m*
warrant (n) *(document)* warrant *m*
warrant (v) *(guarantee)* garantir
warranty garantie *f*
wastage pertes *fpl*, gaspillage *m*
waste (n) déchets *mpl*; gaspillage *m*
waste (v) *(use too much)* gaspiller
waybill lettre *f* de voiture
wear and tear usure *f* normale

weekly hebdomadaire, par semaine
weigh peser
weight poids *m*
weighted index indice pondéré
whole-life insurance assurance *f* vie entière
wholesale (adv) en gros
wholesale discount remise *f* de gros
wholesaler grossiste *m/f*
win a contract remporter un contrat
wind up (a company) liquider une société
window display étalage *m*
withdraw *(money; offer)* retirer
witness (n) témoin *m*
witness (v) *(a document)* signer en qualité de témoin
word-processing traitement *m* de texte
work (n) travail *m*; (v) travailler
work in progress travail en cours
work permit carte *f*/permis *m* de travail
working conditions conditions *f* de travail
worldwide (adj) mondial(e)
worth, be valoir
wrap up *(discussion)* terminer, mettre fin à; *(goods)* emballer
writ injonction *f*
write down *(assets)* réduire la valeur; amortir
write off *(debt)* passer par profits et pertes
write out a cheque/check établir/ libeller un chèque, faire un chèque
write-off *(loss)* perte *f* sèche
written agreement convention écrite, contrat écrit

X, Y, Z

yearly payment paiement annuel, versement annuel
yellow pages pages *f* jaunes (de l'annuaire des téléphones)
yield (n) *(on investment)* rendement *m*
yield (v) *(interest)* rapporter
zip code code *m* postal

French–English Business Dictionary

f	feminine
m	masculine
pl	plural
(adj)	adjective
(v)	verb
qch.	quelque chose
qqn	quelqu'un
so.	someone
sth.	something

A

à l'heure, à temps on time
abattement *m* **(fiscal)** tax allowance
abîmer damage (v)
aboutir à result in
abri *m* **fiscal** tax shelter
accaparer le marché corner the market
accepter accept, take
accepter de faire qch. agree to do sth.
accompagnateur (-trice) courier
accord *m* agreement, contract, deal
accord de longue date long-standing agreement
accord-type *m* model agreement
accoster berth, dock *(of ship)*
accroissement *m* gain *(getting bigger)*
accumuler, s' accrue
accuser réception d'une lettre acknowledge receipt of a letter
achat *m* purchase, purchasing
achat à crédit/à tempérament hire purchase (HP)
achat à terme forward buying
achat (au) comptant cash purchase
achat en gros bulk buying
achats centralisés central purchasing
acheter buy, purchase
acheter à terme buy forward
acheteur (-euse) buyer, shopper, purchaser
acheteur potentiel prospective buyer
acheteur sérieux genuine purchaser
achevé(e) finished, complete
acompte *m* interim payment

acompte, en on account
acquéreur *m* purchaser
acquérir purchase, buy
(coût d')acquisition d'immobilisations capital expenditure
acquitter une traite honour/honor a bill
acte *m* document, deed
acte de vente bill of sale
actif *m* asset
actif circulant current assets
actifs corporels tangible assets
action *f* share/stock *(in a company)*
actionnaire *m/f* shareholder
actionnaire important major shareholder
actionnaire majoritaire/minoritaire majority/minority shareholder
actions *fpl* shareholding
actions ordinaires ordinary shares, equities
actions privilégiées preference shares
activer (une commande) chase (an order)
activité *f* **secondaire** sideline
actuel (-elle) present *(now)*
addition *f* bill *(in a restaurant)*
adjoint(e) deputy
adjuger un contrat à qqn award a contract to so.
administrateur (-trice) (non-executive) director
administrateur judiciaire receiver
administration *f* administration, management
administration, l' the management
adresse de l'expéditeur return address
adresse de réexpédition forwarding address
adresse du bureau/du lieu de travail business address
adresse personnelle home address
adresser une lettre/un colis address a letter/a parcel
aérien, frais *mpl*/**tarifs** *mpl* **de transport** air freight charges/rates
affacturage *m* factoring
affacturage, société d' factor
affaire *f* bargain, deal
affaires, pour on business
affaires *fpl* business

affecter des fonds à un projet

affecter des fonds à un projet earmark funds for a project

affranchir stamp (v) *(a letter)*

affranchir, machine à franking machine

affréter un avion charter an aircraft

agence agency branch (of a bank)

agence de publicité advertising agency

agence de recouvrement (de dettes) debt collection agency

agenda *m* **de poche** pocket diary

agent *m* **de change** stockbroker

agent immobilier estate agent

agios *mpl* bank charges

agir take action

ajournement *m* postponing; adjournment

ajourner postpone, hold over; adjourn

ajouter 10% pour le service add on/allow 10% for service

aller chercher collect, fetch

amende *f* fine

amende, condamner qqn à une fine (v) so.

amortir (un coût) write down (assets)

amortir (un prêt/une dette) amortize (a loan/a debt)

amortir (une dette) redeem (a debt)

amortissement *m* amortization; redemption *(of a debt)*

amortissement linéaire straight line depreciation

analyse des coûts cost analysis

analyse des tâches/de la fonction job analysis

analyse du marché market analysis

analyste *m* **de systèmes, informaticien-analyste** *m* systems analyst

année civile calendar year

année fiscale tax year

année, chaque annually

année, par per annum, per year

annexe *f* appendix

annonce *f* advertisement

annonces classées, petites annonces classified advertisements

annonceur *m* advertiser

annoncer un poste advertise a vacancy

annuaire *m* **des téléphones** telephone directory

annulation *f* **d'un rendez-vous** cancellation of an appointment

annulé(e) cancelled

annuler cancel, revoke

annuler une affaire call off a deal

antidater backdate

appareil *m* **de démonstration** demonstration model

appel *m* **(d'un jugement)** appeal (against a decision)

appel (téléphonique) phone call

appel (téléphonique) en PCV reverse charge call/collect call

appel (venant) de l'extérieur incoming call

appel, prendre un take a call

appeler (au téléphone) phone, telephone, call

appeler en PCV make a reverse charge call, call (v) collect

application *f* implementation

appliquer un accord implement an agreement

appréciation *f* appreciation *(in value)*

apprécier, s' appreciate, increase in value

apprenti(e) trainee

approuver approve, agree

approuver les termes d'un contrat approve the terms of a contract

approvisionner supply (v)

appuyer back up, support

arbitrer un conflit arbitrate in a dispute

archives *fpl* records

argent *m* money

argent comptant (ready) cash

arrêt *m* breakdown, failure

arrêt des paiements suspension of payments

arrêter stop *(doing sth.)*

arrêter le travail stop work, knock off

arrêter les négociations break off negotiations

arrêter un plan d'action decide on a course of action

arrhes *fpl* deposit *(paid in advance)*

arrhes non remboursables non-refundable deposit

arriéré *m* arrears

arrivage *m* consignment

arrivées *fpl* arrivals

arriver arrive, take place

arriver à manage to
arriver à l'hôtel check in (at hotel)
arriver à quai dock (of ship)
arriver à un accord reach an agreement
arriver à un compromis compromise
arriver à une impasse deadlock (v)
arrondir au chiffre inférieur/supérieur round down/up
article m article, clause, item
article imparfait reject
article-réclame m loss-leader
articles de second choix/déclassés seconds
articles divers sundries
articles manufacturés manufactured goods
assemblée générale annuelle annual general meeting (AGM)
assistante de direction personal assistant (PA)
assister à attend (a meeting)
association f association, council; partnership
associé(e) (adj) associate
associé(e) m/f associate, partner
assurance f insurance, (life) assurance
assurance (contre l')incendie fire insurance
assurance tous risques all-risks policy, comprehensive insurance
assurance-vie f life assurance
assurance, attestation f provisoire d' cover note
assurances, compagnie f d' insurance company, insurer
assurer insure, assure
assurer, s'assurer to take out an insurance
assureur m insurer, insurance company
atelier m **de réparation** service centre/center
atout m plus factor
atteindre un objectif meet a target
attendu(e) due (awaited)
attente, en pending
atterrir land (of plane)
attirer appeal to, attract
aubaine f good value (for money); bargain
audit m audit, auditor

audit externe/interne external/internal audit
auditeur m auditor
augmentation f gain/rise/increase in value
augmentation annuelle moyenne mean annual increase
augmentation de salaire pay rise
augmentation en valeur appreciation (in value)
augmenter increase, raise, rise, mark up (the price), expand
augmenter en valeur appreciate, increase in value
augmenter suivant un barème scale up
autorisation f authorization, permission
autoriser license, authorize, permit
autoriser le paiement authorize payment
autoriser une ligne de crédit open a line of credit
autorité f authority
avance f advance (loan), advance (on account), money up front
avance de caisse cash advance, float
avance remboursable refundable deposit
avancer (de l'argent) advance, lend (money)
avant-projet m draft (plan), rough plan
avantage m **spécifique d'un produit** unique selling point (USP)
avantageux (-euse) economical
avaries f average (insurance)
avenant m endorsement (on insurance)
avion-cargo m freight plane
avion, tarifs mpl **de transport par** air freight charges/rates
avis m note, notification
avis d'exécution contract note
avis d'expédition advice note
avocat(e) lawyer
avoir m asset
avoir (v) de l'importance matter (v)
avoir (v) en stock carry/have in stock
avoir fiscal tax credit
avoir lieu, arriver take place
ayant droit m beneficiary

bagages à main

B

bagages à main hand luggage
bail *m* lease
bailleur, bailleresse lessor
bailleur *m* **de fonds** sleeping partner
baisse *f* decrease, drop, fall, downturn
baisse, en decreasing (adj)
baisser drop, fall, decrease
balance *f* **commerciale bénéficiaire/ excédentaire** favourable/favorable balance of trade
banque d'affaires merchant bank
banque de compensation clearing bank
banque (à/au), avoir un compte en have a bank account (with)
barème *m* **fixe** fixed scale of charges
barrer un chèque cross a cheque/ check
barrières *fpl* **douanières** tariff barriers
base *f* **de données** database
base, de basic, most important
bassin *m* dock
bâtiment *m* **principal** main building
bénéfice *m* earnings, profit
bénéfice après impôts after-tax profit, profit after tax
bénéfice avant impôts pretax profit, profit before tax
bénéfice brut gross profit
bénéfice commercial operating profit
bénéfice d'exploitation trading profit
bénéfice net clear profit, net profit
bénéfice théorique paper profit
bénéfices d'une société corporate profits
bénéficiaire *m/f* beneficiary, payee
bénéficier de benefit from, capitalize on
besoins *mpl* requirements
besoins en effectifs manning levels
biens *mpl* **d'équipement** capital equipment, capital goods
biens de consommation consumer goods
biens immobiliers real estate
biens matériels tangible assets
bilan *m* balance sheet
bilan de fin d'exercice closing balance

bilan de vérification trial balance
bilan initial opening balance
billet, prix du fare
billet à ordre promissory note
billet de banque banknote
billet gratuit, billet de faveur complimentary ticket
billetterie *f* cash dispenser
bloqué, fonds *mpl* frozen assets
bloquer des capitaux lock up capital
bloquer les prix peg/freeze prices
bon *m* (government) bond
bon de caisse certificate of deposit
bon (d'échange) voucher
bon du Trésor government bond
bon marché cheap
bon-cadeau *m* gift voucher
bonne affaire good buy
bonne qualité good quality
bonus *m* no-claims bonus
bordereau *m* slip (of paper)
bordereau d'expédition consignment note, dispatch note
bordereau de versement deposit slip, paying-in slip
Bourse *f* **(des valeurs)** stock market, Stock Exchange
bourse de commerce/des matières premières commodity exchange
boutique *f* **hors taxe** duty-free shop
brevet *m* patent
brevet déposé, demande de patent applied for, patent pending
brut gross
brut, faire un profit make a gross profit, gross (v)
budget commercial/des ventes sales budget
budget publicitaire/de publicité advertising budget
budgéter, budgétiser budget (v)
bulletin *m* **de livraison** delivery note
bureau *m* department *(in office)*; desk, office
bureau d'accueil reception desk
bureau d'études design department
bureau de change bureau de change
bureau de renseignements information bureau
bureau paysager/à modules open-plan office
but *m* aim
but (de), avoir pour aim (to)

C

cabinet-conseil *m* consultancy firm
cachet *m* **de la poste** date stamp
cadeau *m* gift, present; premium offer, free gift
cadre *m* executive
cadre moyen middle manager
cadre supérieur senior manager, senior executive
cadres, les management
cadres moyens middle management
cadres supérieurs top management
CAF (coût, assurance, fret) c.i.f. (cost, insurance and freight)
cahier *m* **des charges** specification
caisse *f* case; float; cash desk, checkout *(in supermarket)*
caisse noire hidden reserves
caissier (-ière) cashier
calcul *m* calculation
calculatrice *f* calculator
calculer calculate
calculette *f* calculator
cale *f* hold *(in ship)*
calendrier *m* timetable (of appointments)
campagne *f* **commerciale/de vente(s)** sales campaign
canaux *mpl* **de distribution** channels of distribution
candidature *f* (job) application
candidature (à un poste), poser sa apply for a job
capacité *f* capacity *(ability, production, space)*
capacité d'entreposage storage capacity
capital d'emprunt loan capital
capital initial, capital d'investissement initial capital
capital-risque *m* risk capital, venture capital
capitaliser capitalize
capitaux *mpl* **propres** equity capital
cargaison *f* cargo
carnet *m* **de chèques** cheque/check book
carnet de rendez-vous appointments book; diary
carte *f* **(professionnelle)** (business) card
carte accréditive charge card

carte d'abonnement season ticket
carte de crédit credit card
carte de retrait cash card
carte de travail work permit
carton *m* cardboard box, carton
cas *m* **de force majeure** act of God
cash *m* (ready) cash, spot cash
cash-flow actualisé discounted cash flow (DCF)
casser les prix slash prices
catalogue *m* catalogue/catalog, (price) list
catalogue de vente par correspondance mail-order catalogue/catalog
cause de, à owing to
cautionner to stand guarantee
cautionner qqn bail so. out
centre commercial shopping centre/center
centre de coût cost centre/center
centre de profit profit centre/center
certificat d'action(s) share certificate
certificat d'homologation certificate of approval
certificat de dépôt certificate of deposit
cessation *f* **de paiements** default on payments
cesser stop *(doing sth.)*
cesser (la fabrication/la vente d'un produit) discontinue (a product)
cession-bail *m* lease-back
chambre *f* **d'hôtel** room, hotel room
chambre froide cold store
change *m* foreign exchange
changement *m* change
changement de propriétaire/de direction under new management
changer (de l'argent) change (money)
changer de propriétaire change hands
chapardage *m* pilferage, pilfering
chargement *m* shipment; loading
charger (un programme) load (v) (a computer program)
charger un camion/un navire load a truck/a ship
chariot *m* **élévateur** fork-lift truck
chef de la fabrication production manager
chef de projet project manager

chef de rayon

chef de rayon departmental manager
chef de service head of department, manager
chef des ventes sales manager
chemin *m* **de fer** rail, railway
chèque *m* cheque/check
chèque barré crossed cheque/check
chèque en blanc blank cheque/check
chèque-cadeau *m* gift voucher
chèque, faire un write out a cheque/check
chéquier *m* cheque/check book
cher (chère) dear, expensive
chercheur (-euse) researcher
chiffre *m* figure
chiffre d'affaires turnover; sales figures
chiffre d'affaires de, faire un turn over
chiffres *mpl* figures, statistics
chiffres d'origine historical figures
chiffres réels actuals
choisir choose
choix *m* choice
choix, de premier best quality *(food)*
choix, de second good quality *(food)*; seconds *(articles)*
chômage *m* unemployment
chômage, au/en out of work, unemployed
chute *f* drop, fall
chuter drop (v), plummet
circulaire *f* circular
clair(e) clear, easy to understand
classe *f* **affaires** business class
classe touriste economy class
classer classify; file *(documents)*
classeur *m* filing cabinet
clause *f* article, clause; provision, condition
clause d'abandon waiver clause
clause de résiliation termination clause
clause échappatoire escape clause
clause interdisant la grève no-strike agreement, no-strike clause
clause résolutoire cancellation clause
clavier numérique numeric keypad
claviste *m* keyboarder
client potentiel prospect, prospective customer
clôturer un compte close an account
code *m* **(à) barres** bar code

codirecteur (-trice) général(e) joint managing director
coefficient *m* **de capitalisation des résultats** price/earnings ratio
coentreprise *f* joint venture
coffre-fort *m* safe
colis *m* parcel
combler un manque fill a gap
comité *m* committee, board
comité de conciliation arbitration tribunal
commande *f* order *(for goods)*
commande de réapprovisionnement repeat order, reorder
commande non exécutée unfulfilled order
commande urgente rush order
commandé(e) on order
commande, en on order
commander order (v) *(goods)*
commandes anticipées dues
commandes en attente outstanding orders, back orders
commanditaire *m* sleeping partner
commanditaire sponsor
commanditer sponsor (v)
commerçant(e) trader
commerce extérieur external trade, overseas trade
commerce licite lawful trade
commercialisation *f* marketing
commercialiser un produit market a product
commerciaux *mpl* sales people
commissaire *m* **aux comptes** auditor
commission *f* commission *(money)*; board, committee
commission arbitrale arbitration board
communication *f* phone call
communication urbaine local call
communiqué *m* **de presse** press release
compagnie *f* company, corporation
compagnie d'assurances insurance company
comparer compare
compenser un chèque clear a cheque/check
compétent(e) efficient; experienced
complet (-ète) complete, full
composer un numéro dial a number
comprendre consist of, include

compression f **des dépenses** retrenchment

compris(e) inclusive

comptabilité f bookkeeping; accountancy, accounting

comptant, (au) cash (adv)

compte m account

compte à découvert overdrawn account

compte bloqué account on stop/hold; escrow account

compte courant current account

compte crédit budget account (in bank)

compte créditeur account in credit

compte d'épargne savings account

compte de contrepartie contra account

compte de dépôt(s)/sur livret deposit account

compte de pertes et profits profit and loss account

compte détaillé detailed account, itemized account

compte gelé frozen account

compte oisif/qui dort dead account

compte, qui travaille à son self-employed

compte de, se rendre realize, understand

compter sur depend on

comptes mpl **clients** accounts receivable, receivables

comptes annuels/de l'exercice annual accounts

comptes fournisseurs accounts payable

comptoir m counter

conception f **de produit** product design

concessionnaire m distributor

conclure (un accord) conclude, clinch (an agreement)

concorder (avec) agree, be the same (as)

concurrence f competition

concurrence déloyale unfair competition

concurrence farouche/vive stiff/keen competition

concurrence, en competing (with), in competition (with)

concurrent(e) competitor

concurrentiel (-elle) competing

condition f condition, state

condition, (acheter) à (to buy) on approval

conditionnement m packing, packaging material

conditionner prepack, prepackage

conditions fpl conditions, terms

confiscation f seizure; forfeiture

confisquer seize; declare forfeit

conformément à l'échantillon as per sample

conformément à la facture as per invoice

conformer à, se comply with

congé m **de maternité** maternity leave

congé légal statutory holiday

conjoncture f **économique** economic trends

connaissement m bill of lading

connecter en réseau network (v) (computers)

conseil m board

conseil d'administration board of directors

conseil d'arbitrage adjudication tribunal

conseil de prud'hommes industrial (arbitration) tribunal

conseiller (v) recommend (action)

conseiller m **fiscal** tax consultant

conseiller juridique legal adviser

consigne f left luggage office

consigne de sécurité safety regulation

consigner record (v)

consommateur (-trice) consumer

consommateur (final) end user

consommer (de préférence) jusqu'au/ à best before, use before

constituer (une société) incorporate, set up (a company)

constructeur m manufacturer, maker

consulter un avocat take legal advice

contacter contact (v)

contenant m container

conteneur m container (for shipping)

conteneurs, mettre (des marchandises) en containerize, put into containers

conteneurs, mise f **en** containerization

conteneurisation

conteneurisation *m* containerization
conteneuriser containerize, put into containers
contenir contain, hold
contenu *m* contents
contingent *m* quota
contingent d'importation import quota
contingenter fix quotas
contracter des dettes incur debts
contracter une assurance take out an insurance
contraire contrary
contrat *m* agreement, contract
contrat à durée déterminée fixed-term contract
contrat de productivité productivity agreement
contrat de sous-traitance subcontract
contrat de vente bill of sale
contrat écrit written agreement
contrat forfaitaire/à prix ferme fixed-price agreement
contrat global package deal
contre-proposition *f* counter-offer
contrefaçon *f (d'un produit breveté)* infringement of patent
contrefaire forge; pirate (v)
contrefaire un produit protégé par un brevet infringe a patent
contrepassation *f* contra entry
contrepasser une écriture contra an entry
contresigner countersign
contribuable *m/f* taxpayer
contributions *f* **(in)directes** (in)direct taxation
contrôle *m* control, test, power, check, examination
contrôle aléatoire random check
contrôle des stocks stock/inventory control
contrôle (d'un marché), prendre le capture (a market)
contrôler inspect, control, test, monitor, check
convention *f* agreement, contract
convention collective sur les salaires collective wage agreement
convention écrite written agreement
convivial(e) user-friendly
convoquer convene

coopter qqn co-opt so.
coordonnées *fpl* particulars
copie *f* copy, duplicate *(of document)*
copie (certifiée) conforme certified (true) copy
correspondance *f* correspondence; connecting flight
corriger amend, correct
cosignataire *m/f* joint signatory
cour *f* **(de justice)** court
courant(e) normal, usual
courir accrue
courrier *m* post, mail, letters
courrier au départ outgoing mail
courrier électronique e-mail, electronic mail
cours *m* course; rate, price
cours d'initiation induction courses, induction training
cours de clôture closing price
cours de management/de gestion d'entreprise management course
coursier *m* courier *(messenger)*
court de, à short of
court terme, à short-term (adj)
courtier *m* **d'assurances** insurance broker
coût, assurance, fret (CAF) cost, insurance and freight (c.i.f.)
coût de la main-d'œuvre labour/labor costs
coût de la vie cost of living
coût de revient (des marchandises vendues) cost of sales
coût majoré cost plus
coût unitaire unit cost
coûter cost (v)
coûteux (-euse) dear, expensive, highly priced
coûts d'exploitation operating costs, running costs
coûts opérationnels operating costs, running costs
couvert *m (restaurant)* cover charge
couverture *f* (insurance) cover
couvrir ses dépenses cover costs
créance *f* **douteuse** bad debt
créances *fpl* (outstanding) debts; accounts receivable, receivables
créancier *m* creditor
créancier différé deferred creditor
créancier privilégié secured creditor

créancier sans garantie unsecured creditor
crédit à découvert open credit
crédit à long terme extended credit; long credit
crédit d'impôt tax credit
crédit gratuit interest-free credit
crédit permanent/renouvelable revolving credit
crédit-bail *m* leasing
crédit, à on credit
créditer un compte credit (v) an account
créditeur, compte account in credit
créer une société set up a company
créneau *m* **sur le marché** gap in the market, market opportunity; niche
croissance *f* growth

D

DAB (distributeur automatique de billets) cash dispenser
date d'échéance maturity date
date d'échéance du remboursement redemption date
date d'expiration expiry date
date de livraison delivery date
date limite closing date; deadline
date limite de vente sell-by date
dater (v)
débarquer des marchandises dans un port land goods at a port
débarrasser de qch., se get rid of, dispose of sth.
débit *m* debit
débiter un compte debit an account
débiteur *m* debtor
débiteur condamné à rembourser une dette judgment debtor
débrayer stop work, knock off
décharger unload *(goods)*
déchets *mpl* waste
décision *f* ruling
décision, prendre une reach a decision
déclaration *f* **de revenus** tax return, tax declaration
déclaration sous serment affidavit
déclarer rule, give a decision
décoller take off *(plane)*
décommander un rendez-vous cancel a meeting

décompter deduct
découler de result from
découvert *m* overdraft
découvert autorisé agreed overdraft; open credit
décroissant(e) decreasing (adj)
dédommagement *m* compensation, indemnification *(for damage)*
dédommager compensate, indemnify
dédouanement *m* customs clearance
déductible (des impôts) tax-deductible
déduire deduct
défaillance *f* breakdown, failure
défaillant(e) defaulter
défaut *m* **(de fabrication)** defect
défectueux (-euse) defective, faulty, imperfect
défendre en justice, se defend a lawsuit
déficit commercial trade deficit, trade gap
dégâts *mpl* damage
dégâts causés par le feu fire damage
dehors des heures de pointe, en off-peak
déjeuner *m* **d'affaires** business lunch
délai *m* time scale
délai de livraison delivery time
délai de paiement deferment of payment
délai de réflexion cooling off period
délégué(e) commercial(e) representative, salesman
délit *m* **d'initié(s)** insider dealing
demande *f* claim; inquiry; demand *(for payment)*; request
demander ask for, charge *(money)*, request
demander des renseignements supplémentaires ask for further details
demander un remboursement ask for a refund
démarchage *m* canvassing; door-to-door selling
démarquer mark down
démesuré(e) excessive
demi(e) half (adj)
démissionner resign

démodé(e)

démodé(e) old-fashioned, out of date

déni *m* **de responsabilité** disclaimer

denrée *f* commodity

denrées *fpl* **périssables** perishable goods/items

départs *mpl* departures

départs naturels natural wastage

dépassé(e) old-fashioned, out of date

dépasser exceed

dépasser son budget overspend one's budget

dépense *f* expense, expenditure, outlay

dépenser spend *(money)*

dépenses *fpl* outgoings

déposant(e) depositor

dépositaire *m/f* stockist

dépôt *m* deposit *(in bank)*; store, storeroom, depot

dépôt à terme time deposit

déprécier, se depreciate, lose value

dernier (-ière) last; latest

dernier rappel final demand

description *f* particulars

description *f* **de la fonction** job description

dessin *m* **industriel** industrial design

détail *m* detail; breakdown *(of items)*

détaillant(e) retailer

détails *mpl* particulars

détermination *f* **(de l'assiette fiscale)** (tax) assessment

déterminer un prix price (v), set a price

dette *f* debt

dettes *fpl* accounts payable; liabilities

dettes à court terme current liabilities

dettes à payer outstanding debts

dévaluation *f* devaluation; depreciation

développer, se expand

devis *m* quotation, quote *(estimate of cost)*

devise *f* **(étrangère)** foreign currency

devise faible soft currency

devise forte hard currency, strong currency

devoir owe

DG (directeur (-trice) général(e)) MD (managing director)

diagramme circulaire pie chart

diagramme en bâtons bar chart

différer differ

différer le paiement defer payment

diffuseur *m* distributor

diffusion *f* distribution

diminuer cut, reduce, decrease

diminution *f* decrease

directeur (-trice) (company) director, executive; manager

directeur (-trice) adjoint(e) assistant manager, deputy manager

directeur (-trice) commercial(e) sales executive, sales manager

directeur (-trice) d'agence (bank) branch manager

directeur (-trice) de succursale branch manager

directeur (-trice) général(e) (DG) managing director (MD); general manager

directeur (-trice) général(e) adjoint(e) joint managing director

directeur intérimaire acting manager

directeur régional area manager

direction *f* management

direction générale top management

direction, la the management

directive *f* guideline

directoire *m* board of directors

dirigeant *m* executive

diriger run, manage, direct

diriger une entreprise run a business

discuter discuss; bargain, haggle

disponibilité *f* availability

disponibilités liquid assets

disponible available, obtainable

disque dur hard disk

disquette de sauvergarde backup disk

distribuer (des marchandises) distribute (goods)

distributeur *m* distributor

distributeur automatique de billets (DAB) cash dispenser

divers(e) miscellaneous

dommage *m* damage

dommages-intérêts *mpl*, **dommages et intérêts** damages

données *fpl* data

donner de l'avancement promote *(so.)*

donner en sous-traitance subcontract (v)

donner un contrat à qqn award a contract to so.

dossier m file, dossier, documents

dossiers mpl records

doter en capital capitalize

douane f customs

douanier m customs official

double m duplicate

double imposition double taxation

doubler double (v)

douzaine f

douze douzaines gross (144)

droit m charge, dues; (admission) fee; law; entitlement, right; duty, tax

droit commercial commercial law

droit d'auteur copyright

droit d'enregistrement, droit d'inscription registration fee

droit de passage right of way

droit de retention lien

droit de timbre stamp duty

droit des contrats et obligation contract law

droit(e) right (not left)

droits acquis vested interest

droits d'auteur royalties

droits de douane customs duty

droits de régie excise duty

dû, due due, owing

due, somme amount owing, balance owing

duplicata m duplicate

durée f period, term (of validity)

durée de conservation d'un produit shelf life of a product

durer run, be in force

E

ébauche f draft (plan), rough plan

ébauche de contrat, faire une draft (v) a contract

écart m discrepancy

échange m exchange, swap

échantillon m sample, swatch

échantillon aléatoire random sample

échantillon gratuit free sample

échantillonnage m sampling, testing

échéance f (date of) maturity

échéance, venir à fall (v) due

échelle f **de prix fixe** fixed scale of charges

échelon national, à l' nationwide

échelonner (paiements/vacances) stagger (payments/holidays)

économie f economy (saving)

économie mixte mixed economy

économie parallèle/non officielle black economy

économies, faire des save (v)

économies d'échelle economies of scale

économiser save (v)

économiser l'énergie, qui energy-saving (adj)

écouler le surplus de stock dispose of excess stock

écran m **(d'ordinateur)** monitor (screen)

écrit(e) à la main handwritten

écrit, mettre par put in writing

écriture f entry (writing)

écriture de contrepartie contra entry

écrouler, s' collapse (v)

écu/ECU m ecu, ECU (European currency unit)

effectuer effect (v), make, realize

effet m effect

effet (de commerce) (commercial) bill, instrument

effet à longue échéance long-dated bill

effet de levier gearing, leverage

effet négociable negotiable instrument

effets à payer bills payable

effets à recevoir bills receivable

efficace effective, efficient

efficacité f effectiveness, efficiency

effondrement m collapse

effondrement des ventes slump in sales

effondrer, s' collapse (v)

élever à, s' amount to, total

emballage m packing, packaging material

emballage hermétique airtight packaging

emballage perdu/non consigné non-returnable packing

emballer pack, wrap up (package)

embaucher du personnel hire staff, take on staff

émetteur

émetteur m (d'un chèque) drawer (of a cheque/check)

émettre une lettre de crédit issue a letter of credit

émission prioritaire rights issue

empaqueter pack, wrap up (package)

emplacement m site

emploi m appointment, post, job; employment; use

emploi du temps timetable (of appointments)

employé(e) employee, worker

employé(e) aux écritures bookkeeper

employé(e) de bureau clerk

employé(e) subalterne junior clerk

emprunt m loan; borrowing

emprunt garanti secured loan

emprunter borrow

emprunteur (-euse) borrower

encadrement m du crédit credit freeze

encaisser un chèque cash a cheque/check

encart m publicitaire magazine insert

enchère f auction

endetter, s' get into debt

endommager damage (v)

endosser un chèque endorse a cheque/check

enfreindre la loi break the law

engagement m agreement, commitment

engager (des dépenses) incur (costs)

enlèvement m collection (of goods)

enquête f sur la solvabilité d'un client status inquiry

enregistrement m check-in (counter); (share) registration

enregistrement, bureau d' registry

enregistrer enter, register, record

enseigne f sign

entamer des discussions enter into/initiate discussions

entente f understanding

entente verbale verbal agreement

entrée f entry; admission charge/fee

entreposage m storage, warehousing

entreposer warehouse, store, keep in a warehouse

entrepôt m store, storeroom, warehouse

entrepôt frigorifique cold store

entreprendre embark on

entrepreneur m entrepreneur; contractor

entrepreneur, d' entrepreneurial

entreprise f business, company, enterprise

entreprise de taille moyenne middle-sized company

entreprise mal gérée neglected business

entreprise, dans l' in-house

entretenir maintain (keep going)

entretien m interview; maintenance, service (of machine)

entretien avec (un candidat), avoir un interview so. (v) (for a job)

environ approximately

envoi m consignment, shipping, dispatch, shipment; delivery

envoyer ship, send

envoyer par avion airmail (v)

envoyer par fax/par télécopie fax (v)

envoyer par la poste post, mail

épuisé(e) out of stock

équilibrer balance (v)

équipe f shift, team (of workers)

équipe dirigeante/de direction management team

équiper equip

erreur f discrepancy; error, slip, mistake

erreur aléatoire random error

erreur d'écriture clerical error

erreur de calcul miscalculation

erreur d'ordinateur/faite par l'ordinateur computer error

escompte m discount

escompte m de caisse cash discount

espace m publicitaire advertising space

espèces fpl (ready) cash

esquisse f draft (plan), rough plan

essai, à l' on approval

essentiel (-elle) basic, most important

estampille f de qualité kite mark, quality control stamp

estimation approximative rough estimate, guesstimate

estimer estimate, value; calculate

établir establish
établir un chèque write out a cheque/check
établir une facture make out an invoice
établissement m establishment, business
étage m floor, storey/story
étagère f shelf
étalage m (window) display; display stand
étaler stagger
État m Government
état m condition, state; register, official list; situation, state of affairs
état civil (civil) status
état néant nil return
étayer back up, support
étiqueter label (v)
étiquette f label
étiquette de prix price label/tag
étranger, à l' abroad
étude f de marché market research
étude, bureau d' design department
évaluation f evaluation, assessment, estimate, valuation
évaluer value, evaluate, assess
évasion f fiscale tax avoidance, tax evasion
éventail m de produits product mix
examen m examination (inspection)
examiner check (v)
excédent m glut, surplus
excédent de bagages excess baggage
excédents de stock overstocks
excéder exceed
exception de, à l' excluding
exceptionnel (-elle) outstanding
exclusif, agent/concessionnaire sole agent
exécuter une commande deal with/ fulfil an order
exécution f de commandes order fulfilment
exempter exempt (v)
exercice m financier financial year
exonération f d'impôt exemption from tax, tax exemption
exonéré(e) d'impôt exempt from tax, free of tax
exonérer exempt (v)

expédier (des marchandises) dispatch, send, ship (goods)
expédier par avion airfreight (v)
expéditeur (-trice) sender; shipper
expédition f dispatch, sending, shipping; consignment, shipment
expédition, bordereau m d' dispatch note
expérience f professionnelle track record
expert m consultant, expert; surveyor
expertise valuation; survey
expertiser survey; value (v)
expiration f expiry
expiration, venir à expire
expirer expire, lapse
exploitation f enterprise; exploitation (of labour/labor)
exploiter capitalize on, exploit
exportateur m exporter
exportation f export
exporter export (v)
exposant m exhibitor
exposer exhibit (v)
exposition f exhibition
expropriation f compulsory purchase

F

FAB (franco à bord) f.o.b. (free on board)
fabricant m manufacturer, maker
fabrication f production
fabrication en série mass production
fabrique f factory
fabriquer manufacture (v)
fabriquer des voitures en série mass-produce (v) cars
facilité f (credit) facility
facilités de paiement easy terms
facteur décisif deciding factor
facteur pessimiste/négatif downside factor, minus factor
facteurs conjoncturels cyclical factors
factice, emballage/boîte dummy pack
factor m factor (person, company)
factoring, société f de factor
facture f bill, invoice
facture avec TVA VAT invoice

facture d'avoir

facture d'avoir credit note
facture détaillée detailed/itemized invoice
facture, conformément à la/selon as per invoice
facturer bill, invoice (v)
factures impayées unpaid invoices
failli(e) (adj) bankrupt; *m/f* bankrupt
failli(e) non réhabilité(e) undischarged bankrupt
faillite *f* bankruptcy
faillite, causer/entraîner la bankrupt
faillite, faire go bankrupt, fail
faire concorder reconcile
falsification *f* forgery
falsifier forge, falsify
faux *m* fake
faux frais *mpl* incidental expenses
femme d'affaires businesswoman
fermer (un magasin/une usine) close down (a shop/a factory)
fermer à clé lock (v)
fermer un compte close an account
fête *f* légale statutory holiday
fiabilité *f* reliability
fiable reliable
fiche *f* filing card, slip (of paper)
fichier *m* card index
fichier (informatique) computer file
fichier d'adresses address list, mailing list
fidélité *f* à la marque brand loyalty
filiale *f* subsidiary (company)
fin *f* end
fin, prendre end (v)
financement *m* financing
financer finance, fund (v)
financier (-ière) financial
firme *f* business, company, firm
fixé(e) set (adj)
fixe, barème *m*/**échelle** *f* **de prix** fixed scale of charges
fixer un prix set a price
fixer une réunion à 15h fix a meeting for 3 p.m.
florissant(e) flourishing
fluctuer fluctuate
flux *m* **de trésorerie** cash flow
foire *f* commerciale trade fair
fonction de, en depending on
fonctionnaire *m* official
fondé *m* de pouvoir attorney
fonder establish

fonds *mpl* fund
force majeure, cas de act of God
forfait *m* flat rate; package deal
former qqn train/teach so.
formulaire *m* form
formulaire de candidature/de demande job application form
formulaire de déclaration de douane customs declaration form
fournir supply (v)
fournisseur *m* supplier
fourniture *f* supply
frais *mpl* charge, expense, costs
frais bancaires bank charges
frais généraux/d'administration générale running costs, overheads
frais d'entrepôt storage (cost)
frais de débarquement landing charges
frais de démarrage/d'établissement start-up costs
frais de gestion administrative expenses
frais de manutention handling charges
frais de port et d'emballage postage and packing (p & p)
frais de représentation expense account
frais de transport freight costs, shipping charges, shipping costs
frais de transport (routier) haulage costs, haulage rates
frais financiers interest charges
frais généraux overhead costs, overheads
frais importants heavy costs, heavy expenditure
frais supplémentaires additional charges, extras
franc *m* franc *(currency)*
franc de port carriage free, post free
franchisage *m* franchising
franco à bord (FAB) free on board
franco de port carriage free, post free
fraude *f* fraud
fraude fiscale tax evasion
frauder le fisc evade tax
fret *m* freight *(carriage)*
fret aérien air freight
fuite *f* de capitaux flight of capital
fusion *f* merger
fusionner merge

G

gagner earn *(money)*
gain *m* earnings, profit
gain net clear profit, net profit
gain théorique paper profit
gamme *f* de produits product line, product mix
gamme de prix scale of charges
gamme, (de) bas de down-market
gamme, (de) haut de up-market
garantie *f* guarantee, (insurance) cover; collateral
garantir guarantee, underwrite
gaspillage *m* wastage, waste
gaspiller waste (v)
gelés, actifs *mpl* frozen assets
geler freeze (v) *(prices)*
général(e) general, across-the-board
généralisé(e) across-the-board
gérant(e) manager *(of branch/shop)*
gérer run, manage, direct
gérer une propriété manage property
gestion *f* administration, management
gestion des stocks stock/inventory control
goulot *m*/goulet *m* d'étranglement bottleneck
grand livre ledger
grand livre des achats bought ledger
grand livre des ventes sales ledger
grand magasin department store
grande surface supermarket, hypermarket
grande taille outsize (OS)
graphique *m* diagram
gratuit(e) free (of charge)
grève *f* strike
grève, faire (la)/se mettre en strike
gréviste *m/f* striker
gros, en wholesale (adv)
grosse *f* gross (144)
grossiste *m/f* wholesaler
grouper batch; consolidate
guerre *f* des prix price war

H

habituel (-elle) regular
hausse *f* increase, rise
hebdomadaire weekly
heure d'enregistrement check-in time

heure d'ouverture opening time
heure de fermeture closing time
heure/homme *f*, heure travaillée man-hour
heure, à l' on time
heures d'ouverture business hours, opening hours
heures de bureau office hours
heures de pointe peak period, rush hour
heures supplémentaires overtime
histogramme *m* bar chart
holding *m* holding company
homme d'affaires businessman
honnête reliable
honoraires *mpl* fee *(for services)*
honorer une traite honour/honor a bill
horaire *m* timetable *(trains, etc.)*
hors tax exclusive of tax, tax-free
hypothèque *f*, prêt *m* hypothécaire mortgage

I

image *f* de marque (de la société) corporate image
immatriculer une société register (v) a company
immobilisations *fpl* incorporelles intangible assets
immobiliser des capitaux lock up capital
impasse *f* deadlock
impayé(e) outstanding, unpaid
implanter sur un marché, s' penetrate a market
importateur (-trice) importer
importation *f* import
importer import (v)
imposer tax (v)
imposition *f* indirecte indirect taxation
impôt *m* tax, levy
impôt normal/de base basic tax
impôt progressif graduated income tax
impôt retenu à la source tax deducted at source
impôt sur le revenu income tax
impôt sur les sociétés corporation tax
imprimante *f* printer *(machine)*

imprimer

imprimer print out
inclure include
inclus(e) inclusive
incompétence f inefficiency
incompétent(e) inefficient
incorporé(e) built-in
indemnisation f indemnification, compensation *(for loss)*
indemniser compensate *(for loss)*
indemnité f indemnity
indemnité de vie chère cost-of-living allowance
indépendant(e) self-employed
indexé(e) index-linked
indexer index (v)
indicateur m timetable *(trains, etc.)*
indicateurs économiques economic indicators
indicatif m **(téléphonique)** dialling code
indicatif de zone area code
indice des prix à la consommation retail price index
indice pondéré weighted index
indiquer specify; show
industrie à fort coefficient de capital capital-intensive industry
industrie clé key industry
industrie de base primary industry
industrie de services service industry, tertiary industry
industrie de transformation secondary industry
industrie en pleine croissance boom industry
industrie principale staple industry
industriel m industrialist
inefficacité f inefficiency
inférieur(e) à under, less than
inflationniste inflationary
informaticien-analyste m systems analyst
informatiser computerize
ingénieur m **de chantier** site engineer
injonction f writ
inoccupé(e) vacant
inscrire enter, write in, register
inscrire à l'arrivée, s' check in
insolvable insolvent
inspecteur m **des impôts** tax inspector
installations fpl facilities

instructions fpl **pour l'expédition** shipping/forwarding instructions
instrument m instrument, document; implement, tool
intégré(e) built-in
intenter un procès à/contre qqn sue
interdiction f ban
interdire ban (v)
intéresser (qqn) interest (so.)
intérêt m interest *(paid on investment)*
intérêt élevé high interest
intérêts mpl vested interest
intérêts (à payer) interest charges
intérêts composés compound interest, cumulative interest
intérim de qqn, assurer l' deputize for so.
intérim, faire de l' temp (v)
intermédiaire m intermediary, middleman
interprète m/f interpreter
interprète, servir d' interpret
intervenir take action
introduire des données input information, data
introduire graduellement phase in
invendus mpl returns *(unsold goods)*
inventaire m inventory, stock list
inventaire (des stocks) stocktaking
inverse reverse (adj)
investissement, faire un invest
isolé(e) one-off

J

jauge f tonnage
jeter après usage, à disposable
joindre contact; join
joindre (à une lettre) enclose
jour m day *(24 hours)*
jour férié bank holiday, public holiday
jour, à up to date
jour, mettre à update (v)
jour, par per day
journal m journal *(accounts book)*
journal professionnel trade journal
journée f **(de travail)** day *(working day)*
jugement m ruling
juridique legal *(referring to law)*
justifier account for

L

lancement m **d'une société en Bourse** flotation

lancer un nouveau produit promote a new product

lancer une société (en Bourse) float a company

lancer dans les affaires, se go into business

leader m market leader

lecteur m **disques/de disquettes** disk drive

lettre d'accompagnement covering letter

lettre de change bill of exchange, draft

lettre de crédit letter of credit (L/C)

lettre de réclamation letter of complaint

lettre de recommendation letter of reference

lettre de relance follow-up letter

lettre de voiture waybill

lettre exprès/prioritaire express letter

lettre recommandée registered letter

levée f **d'une option** exercise of an option

lever (un impôt) levy (a tax)

lever l'embargo lift an embargo

lever la séance close/adjourn the meeting

lever une option exercise an option

libellé m description

libeller un chèque write out a cheque/check

libre free, vacant

licencié(e) redundant, laid-off (staff)

licencié(e), être be made redundant

licenciement m dismissal, redundancy

licencier des ouvriers lay off workers

licencier qqn make so. redundant; dismiss/sack so.

lié par contrat under contract

lieu m **de travail** place of work

ligne f **de conduite** guideline

ligne (téléphonique) extérieure outside line

ligne de produits product line

limite de crédit credit limit, lending limit

limiter limit, restrict

liquidateur m liquidator

liquidation f **d'un société** liquidation

liquidation forcée forced sale

liquide m (ready) cash

liquider du stock liquidate/clear stock

liquider les commandes en attente release dues

liquider une entreprise/une société liquidate/wind up a company

liquidité f liquidity

liquidités fpl liquid assets

liste f register, official list

liste de colisage packing list, packing slip

liste de sélection shortlist

liste noire, mettre sur la blacklist (v)

liste rouge, sur la ex-directory

listing m (computer) printout

livraison f delivery (of goods)

livraison contre remboursement cash on delivery (c.o.d.), payable on delivery

livraison gratuite free delivery

livraison d'un envoi, prendre accept delivery of a shipment

livre f pound (weight, 0.45kg)

livre f **sterling** pound (sterling)

livre m **de caisse** cash book

livre-journal m journal (accounts book)

livrer deliver

livret m **(de banque)** bank book

local m **à usage de bureaux** business premises, office space

locataire m/f tenant

locataire à bail lessee

location-bail f lease

location, prendre en rent

location, prix de rental

locaux mpl premises

logiciel m computer program, software

lot m batch (of products)

louer let; rent (v)

louer à bail lease

louer une voiture hire/rent a car

louer, bureau à office to let

loyer m rent

lucratif, non/sans but non profit-making

M

machines *fpl* plant, machinery
magasin *m* shop; store, storeroom
magasin à succursales multiples chain store, multiple store
magasin, (grand) department store, large shop
mailing *m* mail shot, mailing shot
main-d'œuvre *f* manpower
main-d'œuvre bon marché cheap labour/labor
maintenance *f* maintenance, service
maintenir maintain *(keep going)*
maison *f* firm, house, company
maison de commerce business, firm
maison mère parent company
maison, dans la in-house
maîtrise *f* control, power
majorer mark up
malentendu *m* misunderstanding
mandat *m* order *(money)*
mandat international foreign money order
mandat postal/-poste *m* money order
manœuvre *m* manual worker
manque *m* shortage
manquement *m* default
manquer miss
manquer de run out of
manuel *m* **d'entretien** service manual
manuel d'utilisation operating manual
manuscrit(e) handwritten
maquette *f* dummy, mock-up, model
marchand(e) dealer, merchant, trader
marchander bargain (v)
marchandisage *m* merchandizing
marchandise réimportée reimport
marchandises *fpl* goods
marchandises à prix sacrifiés cut-price goods
marchandises exportées exports
marché *m* market *(possible sales)*; bargain, deal
marché à terme forward market
marché captif captive market
marché ciblé target market
marché d'exclusivité closed market
marché des changes foreign exchange market

marché des matières premières commodity market
marché des valeurs mobilières stock market
marché intérieur domestic market
marché libre open market
marché noir black market
marchés étrangers overseas markets
marge *f* (profit) margin
marge bénéficiaire mark-up, profit margin
marge brute d'auto-financement (MBA) cash flow
marque *f* brand
marque de fabrique/de commerce trademark, trade name
marque déposée registered trademark
marqueur *m* marker pen
masse *f* **monétaire** money supply
matériel *m* equipment
matériel de publicité sur le lieu de vente (PLV) point of sale material
matériel lourd heavy equipment
matériel publicitaire display material
matières *fpl* **premières** raw materials
maturité, arriver à fall due
mauvais payeur slow payer
MBA (marge brute d'auto-financement) cash flow
médias *mpl* (mass) media
médiateur *m* ombudsman
mémoire *f* **(d'ordinateur)** storage *(computer)*
mener des négociations conduct negotiations
mensualités *fpl* monthly payments
mensuel (-elle) monthly (adj)
mentionner refer *(to item)*
menues dépenses petty expenses
mériter earn
mesure *f* **du rendement** measurement of profitability
mesures de sécurité safety precautions
mesures fiscales fiscal measures
méthode *m* **de coûts marginaux** marginal pricing
mettre fin graduellement phase out
mise *f* bid, offer to buy
mise de fonds capital laid out

mobiliser des capitaux mobilize capital
modalités *fpl* **de paiement** modes of payment
mode *m* **d'emploi** directions for use
modèle *m* model, style of product
modèle de démonstration demonstration model
modèle déposé registered design
modèle réduit model *(small copy)*
modéré(e) moderate (adj)
modifier amend
moins de under, less than
moins-value *f* depreciation, loss of value
mois civil/complet calendar month
moitié *f* half
mondial(e) worldwide (adj)
monétaire monetary
monnaie *f* cash; change; currency
monnaie étrangère foreign currency
monnaie stable stable currency
monopole *m* monopoly
montant *m* amount *(of money)*
montant forfaitaire lump sum
montant total total amount
montant total de la facture total invoice value
montant versé amount paid
monter à bord board *(boat, air, train)*; embark *(boat)*
monter à , se amount to, total
moratoire *m* moratorium
morte-saison *f* off-season
motivé(e) motivated
mouiller berth (v)
moyen (-enne) average, medium-sized
moyenne *f* mean, average
moyens *mpl* means *(money)*
moyens frauduleux false pretences

N

N° 1 du marché market leader
nantissement *m* collateral
nation *f* **la plus favorisée** most-favoured/favored nation
national(e) national; nationwide
navire *m* ship
néant *m* nil
négociant(e) dealer, merchant, trader
négociateur (-trice) negotiator

négociations salariales wage negotiations
net, nette net (adj)
net, actif *m* net assets
nette, valeur *f* net worth
niveau *m* level
noliser un avion charter an aircraft
nom *m* **de marque** brand name
nom de, au on behalf of
nombres impairs odd numbers
nombres pairs even numbers
nommer appoint
non daté(e) undated
non disponible unavailable
non-paiement *m* non-payment
normal(e) normal, regular, ordinary, standard
normaliser standardize
norme *f* standard
notaire *m* solicitor; notary public
notation *f*/**note** *f* **financière (d'une société)** credit rating
note *f* note; bill, invoice; memo
note de frais expense account
note de, prendre take note of; minute
noter enter, write in
notifier notify
nouvelle commande *f* reorder, repeat order
nul, nulle null, void, not valid
numéro de boîte postale box number
numéro de commande order number
numéro de facture invoice number
numéro de lot batch number
numéro de série serial number
numéroter number (v)

O

objectif *m* objective, aim, target
objectif de vente sales target
objectifs de production production targets
obligation *f* obligation, duty; (government) bond
obligation (non garantie) debenture
obligation au porteur bearer bond
obligation non remboursable irredeemable bond
obligations spéculatives non garanties junk bonds
obsolescence *f* obsolescence

obtenir

obtenir obtain
occasion f bargain *(cheaper than usual)*
occasion, d' secondhand
occupé(e) busy, engaged *(telephone)*
occuper de (qch.), s' attend to, handle, deal with
officiel (-elle) official, formal
officieux (-euse) unofficial
offre f bid, offer
offre de lancement introductory offer
offre publique d'achat (OPA) takeover bid
offre unique unique selling proposition (USP)
offres d'emploi appointments, situations vacant
offrir offer (v)
onéreux (-euse) highly-priced
OPA (offre publique d'achat) takeover bid
opérateur (-trice) operator
opération f **clés en main** turnkey operation
opposer une demande reconventionnelle counter-claim
opposer à une décision, s' veto a decision
opposition à un chèque, faire stop a cheque/check
option f **d'achat** option to purchase
option, en optional
ordinaire regular, ordinary, standard
ordinateur m computer
ordinateur personnel personal computer (PC)
ordre de virement bancaire banker's order
ordre du jour agenda
organigramme m organization chart; flow chart
organiser arrange, organize
osciller fluctuate
outil m implement
ouvert(e) open (adj) *(not closed)*
ouvriers mpl **qualifiés** skilled workers
ouvriers payés à l'heure hourly-paid workers
ouvriers spécialisés semi-skilled workers
ouvrir la séance open the meeting

P

p.j. (pièce jointe) enclosure (encl.)
pages fpl **jaunes** yellow pages
paie f pay, wage, salary
paiement m settlement, payment
paiement à la livraison cash on delivery (c.o.d.)
paiement anticipé advance payment
paiement (au) comptant cash terms; payment in cash
paiement d'avance prepayment; money up front
paiement en espèces/cash payment in cash
paiement forfaitaire lump sum
paiement intérimaire interim payment
paiements échelonnés staged payments
panne f breakdown, failure
panneau m **publicitaire** sign
PAO (publication assistée par ordinateur) desk-top publishing
paperasserie f paperwork
paperasserie administrative red tape
papiers falsifiés faked documents
paradis m **fiscal** tax haven
parapher initial (v)
parrain m sponsor
parrainage m sponsorship
parrainer sponsor (v)
part f proportion
part du marché market share
partager share
partager un bureau share an office
partenaire m **commercial** trading partner
participation f shareholding
partie f proportion; party *(judicial)*
partie plaignante plaintiff
passer à switch over to
passer par profits et pertes write off
passer une commande place an order
passible de liable to
passif m liabilities
passif exigible current liabilities
patron m boss *(informal)*
pavé m **numérique** numeric keypad
payable à vue/sur présentation payable on demand
payé(e) paid *(invoice)*

payé(e) d'avance prepaid
payer (une facture) settle *(an invoice)*
payer comptant pay cash
payer d'avance pay in advance
payer trop cher be overcharged
payer une note pay a bill
payer, à outstanding, unpaid
payer, sans free (of charge)
payeur *m* payer
pays *m* **d'origine** country of origin
péage *m* toll
pénétrer enter, go in
pénétrer un marché penetrate a market
pension *f* **de retraite** pension
pénurie *f* shortage
pénurie de main-d'œuvre manpower shortage
PEPS (premier entré, premier sorti) FIFO (first in first out)
PER (coefficient de capitalisation des résultats) price/earnings ratio
percepteur *m* tax collector
perception *f* **des impôts** tax collection
percevoir (un impôt) levy (a tax)
perdre de l'argent lose money
perdre des arrhes forfeit a deposit
perdre une commande lose an order
performance *f* efficiency
performant(e) efficient
périmé(e) obsolete
périodique *m* magazine
périphériques *mpl* peripherals
permanence *f* **téléphonique** answering service
permis *m* permit, authorization, licence
permis de séjour residence permit
permis de travail work permit
personne *f* **désignée** nominee
personnel de base skeleton staff
personnel de bureau office staff
personnel de direction managerial staff
personnel réduit skeleton staff
perspectives *fpl* prospects
perte *f* loss *(of sth.)*
perte d'exploitation trading loss
perte de valeur decrease in value
perte sèche dead loss, write-off
perte théorique paper loss
pertes *fpl* wastage

peser weigh
petite caisse petty cash
petites (et moyennes) entreprises (PME) small businesses
petites dépenses petty expenses
pétrole *m* oil *(petroleum)*
PIB (produit intérieur brut) GDP (gross domestic product)
pièce *f* **(de monnaie)** coin
pièce détachée/de rechange spare part
pièce jointe (p.j.) enclosure (encl.)
pied, mettre à lay off
place *f* room, space
placement *m* **(financier)** investment
placement sûr safe investment
placer (de l'argent) invest
plafond *m* **de crédit** credit limit, lending limit
plafond des prix price ceiling
plaindre (de), se complain (about)
plan *m* plan, project, draft
plan d'ensemble floor plan
plan d'urgence contingency plan
plan de développement de la société corporate plan
planifier plan (v)
plein(e) full
plus-value *f* capital gains
PME (petites et moyennes entreprises) small businesses
PNB (produit national brut) GNP (gross national product)
poids *m* weight
poids brut gross weight
poids lourd heavy goods vehicle
poids net net weight
point *m* matter, question
point de vente point of sale
point de vente électronique electronic point of sale (EPOS)
point, mettre au finalize; develop
pointe, de state-of-the-art
police *f* **d'assurance** insurance policy
police d'assurance-vie life assurance policy
politique *f* policy
politique (de fixation) des prix pricing policy
politique générale code of practice
polycopier duplicate (v)
port *m* carriage, freight costs; port *(computer)*; harbour/habor, port

port d'escale

port d'escale port of call
port dû, (en) carriage forward, freight forward
port payé, (en) postpaid, postage paid, carriage paid
port et d'emballage, frais de postage and packing (p & p)
portatif (-ive), portable portable
porte-à-porte m door-to-door selling
porte-documents m briefcase
porte, être mis(e) à la get the sack, be sacked
porte, mettre à la sack (v) so.
portefeuille f (d'actions) portfolio
porter carry, transport
porter intérêt bear (interest)
porteur m bearer
position f status
position d'un compte (bancaire) bank balance
position financière financial position
posséder possess
poste f post, mail, postal system
poste f aérienne airmail
poste f centrale general post office
poste m position, post, job
poste m (téléphonique) extension
poste m clé key post
poste m frontière customs entry point
poste m vacant/à pourvoir vacancy
postes à pourvoir situations vacant
poste, mettre à la post, mail
poster post, mail
pot-de-vin m bribe
pourboire m tip (money)
poursuite f en dommages-intérêts action for damages
poursuites judiciaires prosecution; lawsuit, legal proceedings
poursuivre qqn en justice sue so., prosecute so., take so. to court
pourvu que provided that, providing
pouvoir m d'achat purchasing power
préavis m notice
précision f detail
préemballer prepack, prepackage
prélèvement m deduction
prélèvement automatique direct debit
prélever deduct
premier entré, premier sorti (PEPS) first in first out (FIFO)

prendre des mesures take action
prendre fin expire
préposé(e) booking clerk
présenter (qqn) introduce (so.)
présenter un compte invoice, render an account
présenter une traite à l'acceptation present a bill for acceptance
présenter à l'enregistrement, se check in (at airport)
présenter à un entretien, se report for an interview
présentoir m display stand
président-directeur général (PDG) chairman and managing director, chief executive
prêt m loan
prêt à terme term loan
prêt hypothécaire mortgage
prêt(e) ready
prêter lend
prêter (de l'argent) advance, lend
prêter sur hypothèque mortgage (v)
prêteur m lender
prévention f prevention
prévenu(e) defendant, accused
prévision f forecast
prévisions de trésorerie cash flow forecast
prévisions des ventes sales forecast
prévoir forecast (v)
prime f bonus; premium offer
prime (d'assurance) (insurance) premium
prime d'encouragement merit award, merit bonus
principal(e) chief, principal
principe m principle
prise f de contrôle takeover
prise de position dans les négociations bargaining position
prix m price, rate; charge, cost
prix à la portée de tous popular prices
prix à quai landed costs
prix au comptant spot price
prix avec rabais discount price
prix catalogue catalogue/catalog price, list price
prix concurrentiel/compétitif competitive price
prix convenu agreed price

prix coûtant cost price
prix de clôture closing price
prix de détail retail price
prix de facture invoice value/price
prix de gros trade price
prix de revient de base prime cost
prix de seuil threshold price
prix de soutien support price
prix ex-entrepôt/départ entrepôt
  price ex warehouse
prix départ usine factory price, price
  ex works
prix du billet fare
prix du comptant cash price
prix du transport freight *(carriage)*
prix équitable fair price
prix fort full price
prix imposé set price
prix les plus bas rock-bottom prices
prix livré supply price
prix moyen average price
prix plafond ceiling price
prix réduit cut price
**prix tout compris (port et emballage
  inclus)** delivered price
prix unitaire/de l'unité unit price
prix, citer/donner un quote, estimate
  costs
procès m lawsuit
procès-verbal m minutes
  (of meeting)
procuration f power of attorney
procurer, se obtain
procurer des fonds, se secure funds,
  raise money
production en série mass production
production intérieure domestic
  production
produire un bénéfice show a profit
produit m product
produit d'appel loss-leader
produit dérivé spinoff
produit fini end product
produit grand public mass market
  product
produit intérieur brut (PIB) gross
  domestic product (GDP)
produit national brut (PNB) gross
  national product (GNP)
produits à marque du distributeur
  own label goods, own brand goods
produits concurrentiels competing
  products

profil m **de poste** job description
profiter de benefit from, capitalize on
programme (logiciel) computer
  program, software
programme pilote pilot scheme
programmer un ordinateur
  program (v) a computer
projet m project, plan
projeter plan (v)
prolongation f extension,
  extending
prolongation d'une traite renewal of
  a bill of exchange
prolonger extend, make longer
prolonger une traite renew a bill
  of exchange
promouvoir promote *(so.)*
pronostic m forecast
proportionnel (à la valeur) ad
  valorem
proposer offer
propriétaire m/f owner, proprietor;
  landlord; proprietress
propriétaire légitime rightful owner
propriété f property; ownership
propriété collective collective
  ownership
propriété privée private property
prospect m prospective buyer
prospectus publicitaires junk mail
prospère flourishing
protéger safeguard
provenance f origin
provenir de result from, come
  from
provision f advance (on account);
  deposit *(paid in advance)*
provision, (chèque) sans dud cheque/
  check
provisions fpl reserve *(supplies)*
provisions pour dépréciation
  allowance for depreciation
pub f publicity
publication f **assistée par ordinateur
  (PAO)** desk-top publishing (DTP)
publicité f publicity, advertising;
  advertisement; (TV) commercial
publicité avec coupon-réponse
  coupon ad
publicité de produit product
  advertising
publier release (v) *(make public)*
publipostage m mailing

Q

quai m quay
quai, arriver à berth (v)
qualification f job title
qualifications professionnelles professional qualifications
qualifié(e) qualified (skilled)
qualité, de première first-class, high-quality
quart m quarter (25%)
question f question, matter; business, item (on agenda)
quittance f receipt

R

rabais m discount
rabais de, faire un knock off, reduce a price (by)
rabattre deduct, take off
rachat m takeover
rachat contesté contested takeover
raison de, en owing to
rappel m d'impôt back tax
rapport m report; ratio
rapport annuel annual report
rapport d'avancement du travail progress report
rapport qualité good value
rapport avec, en relating to
rapport, faire un report (v)
rapporter earn, yield (interest)
rapportant à, se relating to
rapporter brut gross (v)
rapprochement m reconciliation
ratage m flop
rater fail, fall through, flop
ratio d'endettement leverage
ratio fonds propres/emprunts gearing
rayer delete
rayon m department (in shop); counter; shelf
rayonnage m shelving (shelves)
réaction f response, reaction
réaliser une propriété/des biens realize property/assets
réapprovisionnement m reorder
réapprovisionner, se reorder (v), restock
réception f receipt (receiving)

réceptionner (des marchandises) receive, accept delivery of (goods)
recettes fpl receipts, takings
receveur m tax collector
recherche f des besoins des consommateurs consumer research
récipient m container
réclamation f complaint, claim; demand (for payment)
réclamer demand (v)
réclamer (des dommages et intérêts) claim (v) (insurance)
recommandation f reference (on person)
recommander recommend (course of action); register (a letter)
reconduire un crédit/une dette roll over credit/a debt
reconnaître officiellement un syndicat recognize a union
recouvrement m de dettes debt collection
recouvrer recover, get sth. back
recouvrer une créance collect a debt
rectifier amend
reçu m receipt
recul m downturn, setback
récupération f recovery, getting back
récupérer recover, get sth. back
recycler qqn, se retrain
redevance f fee (for admission); royalty
rédiger put in writing
rédiger un contrat draw up a contract
rédiger une facture make out an invoice, raise an invoice
réduction f cut; discount
réduire mark down; reduce, cut
réduire la valeur write down (assets)
réduire suivant un barème scale down
réévaluer reassess
référence f reference (on person)
référence, (point de) benchmark
référer à, se refer (to item)
refus m refusal
refuser refuse, turn down, reject
registre m register, official list; ledger
réglage m plus fin/plus précis (de l'économie) fine tuning

règle f rule
réglé(e) paid *(invoice)*
règlement m remittance, payment, settlement
réglementer regulate *(by law)*
règlements mpl regulations
régler (une facture) settle (an invoice)
régler par chèque pay by cheque/check
régler un compte settle an account
régler une note/facture pay a bill/an invoice
régulier (-ière) regular
rejeter reject
relance f revival, recovery
relancer (l'économie) revive (the economy)
relancer chase *(an order)*
relatif à relating to
relation f connection
relations fpl relations
relations entre employeurs et employés industrial relations
relations publiques public relations (PR)
relevé m **de compte** statement of account
relevé de compte bank statement
relever (directement) de qqn report to, be responsible for so.
relier join
reliquat m remainder
remboursable repayable; refundable
remboursement m refund
remboursement (d'un emprunt) redemption (of a loan)
rembourser refund, repay, pay back
rembourser (un prêt/une dette) amortize (a loan)/repay (a debt)
remerciements mpl (vote of) thanks
remettre hold over, postpone
remettre (à qqn) hand over
remettre, se recover, get better
remise f discount
remise à plus tard postponement
remise commerciale trade discount
remise habituelle/de base basic discount
remise de gros wholesale discount

remise professionnelle trade terms, trade discount
remise sur quantité quantity discount, volume discount
remplacement m replacement *(item)*
remporter un contrat win a contract
rémunération f remuneration, salary; fee *(for services)*
rémunérer remunerate
rencontrer meet *(so.)*
rencontrer, se meet
rendement m return, profit; yield; productivity, output, throughput
rendement, à plein at full capacity
rendez-vous m appointment
rendre compte de account for
renoncer à (des droits) waive (a claim)
renouveler un bail renew a lease
renouveler une commande repeat an order, reorder
renouvellement m **d'un abonnement** renewal of a subscription
renseignement(s) m(pl) information
renseignements sur les horaires des vols flight information
renseigner, se inquire
rentabilité f cost-effectiveness, profitability
rentabilité d'un investissement return on investment (ROI)
rentable cost-effective, profitable
rentrée f revenue
rentrer dans ses frais break even (v)
renvoi m postponement
renvoyer qqn sack so.
renvoyer une lettre à l'expéditeur return a letter to sender
réparer make good *(a defect/loss)*; fix, mend *(a machine)*
répartir un risque spread a risk
repas m **d'affaires** business lunch
repère m benchmark
répertoire m **d'adresses** address list
répertoire d'adresses par professions classified directory
répertoire des entreprises trade directory
repli m downturn
répondant m reference, referee

répondeur téléphonique

répondeur *m* **téléphonique** answering machine

répondre à la demande meet/satisfy the demand

réponse à (votre demande), en further to (your inquiry)

reporter put back, postpone

reporter à, se refer *(to item)*

reprendre les négociations resume negotiations

représentant(e) salesman, representative; agent

représentant(e) à la commission commission rep

représentation, faire de la represent *(a company)*

reprise (contre un achat) part exchange, trade-in

reprise *f* recovery *(getting better)*

reproduire copy (v)

réputation *f* standing

requête *f* request

réservation en bloc block booking

réserve *f* reserve *(money)*

réserve, sans unconditional

réserve de, sous on condition that, subject to

réserver book, reserve (v)

réserves *fpl* reserves *(supplies)*

réserves occultes hidden reserves

réserves, faire des stock up

résident(e) resident (adj)

résiliation *f* surrender *(of a policy)*

résilier un contrat cancel a contract, terminate an agreement, call off a deal

résoudre un problème solve a problem

respecter un délai meet a deadline

responsabilité contractuelle contractual liability

responsabilité limitée limited liability

responsable (de) liable (for), responsible (for)

responsable *m/f* head, manager

responsable de clientèle/de gestion de budget account executive

responsable de service head of department

responsable de suivi progress chaser

resquiller dans une queue jump the queue/line

resserrer (le contrôle) tighten up on

reste *m* remainder

rester remain *(be left)*

restriction *f* **du crédit** credit freeze

restructuration *f* **d'un emprunt** restructuring of a loan

résultat *m* effect

résultat quantitatif figures

résultat, avoir pour result in

résultats *mpl* results *(of company)*

retard *m* delay, hold-up

retard, être en/prendre du fall behind, be late

retarder hold up, delay

retenir une chambre reserve a room

retenue *f* **(sur salaire)** deduction (from salary)

retenue à la source deduction at source; withholding tax

retirer withdraw

retours *mpl* returns

retraite, âge *m* **de la** retirement age

retraite, prendre sa/partir à la retire

retrancher deduct

rétribuer remunerate

réunion *f* meeting

réunion du conseil d'administration board meeting

réunion du service commercial sales conference

réunir bracket together

réunir, se meet

réussir succeed, do well

réussir à manage to

réussit, qui successful

réussit pas, qui ne unsuccessful

revendication *f* claim

revente *f* resale

revenu *m* revenue; return, profit; income

revenu fixe fixed income

revenu imposable taxable income

revenus de placements investment income

revenus invisibles invisible earnings

revers *m* setback

réviser update (v) *(data, results)*

réviser (une machine) service (a machine)

révision *f* **de salaire** salary review

révoquer revoke

revue *f* magazine

risque *m* risk, exposure

risque financier financial risk
risque de l'acheteur, aux caveat emptor
risquer risk (v) (money)
ristourne f volume discount
rompre les négociations break off negotiations
rompre un accord/un contrat break an agreement
route f road
rupture f **de contrat** breach of contract
rupture de stock, en out of stock

S

S.A. (société anonyme) Public Limited Company (Plc)
S.A.R.L (société à responsabilité limitée) limited (liability) company
saisie f seizure
saisir seize; input information
saison f season (time of year)
salaire m salary, pay, earnings, wage
salaire brut gross salary
salaire de départ/de débutant starting salary
salaire horaire hourly wage
salarié(e) (adj) salaried
salarié(e) m/f employee
salle de conférences/de réunion conference room
sanctionner penalize
satisfaire (un client) satisfy (a customer)
satisfaire à la demande keep up with/meet/satisfy the demand
saturer le marché saturate the market
sauf erreur ou omission errors and omissions excepted (e. & o.e.)
sauvegarder safeguard; back up, save (computer file)
sauver salvage
sauvetage m salvage (action)
SAV (service après-vente) after-sales service
schéma m diagram
secrétaire (de direction) personal assistant (PA)
secrétaire intérimaire temp
secrétaire particulière PA (personal assistant)

secteur m sector, area; territory; division (part of a company)
secteur difficile problem area
secteur primaire primary industry
secteur secondaire secondary industry
secteur tertiaire service industry
sécurité f safety
sécurité de l'emploi job security, security of employment
séduire appeal to, attract
séjour m residence
sélectionner (des candidats) shortlist (candidates)
selon under, according to
selon échantillon as per sample
semaine, par per week, weekly
semestre m **comptable** half-year
séparé, sous pli under separate cover
serrure f lock
service m department (in office); service; service charge (restaurant)
service achats buying department
service après-vente (SAV) after-sales service
service clients customer service department
service colis (postaux) parcel post
service commercial sales department
service d'entretien service department
service de la comptabilité accounts department
service des réclamations complaints department
service des sinistres/des réclamations claims department
service médiocre poor service
service rapide prompt service
services informatiques computer services
serviette f briefcase
servir de, se use (v)
servitude f right of way
seuil m **de rentabilité** breakeven point
seul propriétaire sole owner
siège m base (place)
siège m **social** main office, head office, HQ, registered office
signaler report (v)

signataire

signataire *m/f* signatory
signer sign (v)
signer de ses initiales initial (v)
situation *f* situation, state of affairs
situation financière financial position
situation légale legal status
société *f* company, corporation
société *f* **exportatrice** exporter
société à responsabilité limitée limited (liability) company (Ltd)
société anonyme Public Limited Company (Plc)
société concurrente rival company
société indépendante independent company
société mère parent company
société opéable takeover target
société sœur sister company
soins de, aux bons care of (c/o)
solde *m* balance; sale *(at a low price)*
solde à ce jour/à reporter balance carried down/carried forward
solde à moitié prix half-price sale
solde à nouveau, ancien solde, solde reporté balance brought down/ brought forward
solde à recevoir/à régler balance due to us
solde créditeur credit balance
solde de trésorerie cash balance
solde dû balance due
solder un compte settle an account
soldes avant inventaire stocktaking sale
solliciter ask for, request
solliciter des commandes solicit orders
solliciter un emploi apply for a job
solvabilité *f* solvency
solvable solvent (adj)
somme *f* sum, amount *(of money)*
somme globale grand total
sondage *m* **d'opinion** opinion poll
sortie *f* **d'imprimante** (computer) printout
sorties *fpl* outgoings
souche *f* counterfoil
soumission *f* tender
soumissions cachetées sealed tenders
souple flexible

souplesse *f* flexibility
source *f* **de revenus** source of income
sous-directeur (-trice) assistant manager
sous-location *f* sublease
sous-louer sublet, sublease (v)
sous-traitance, donner en subcontract (v)
sous-traitant *m* subcontractor
sous-traiter subcontract (v)
souscrire une assurance take out an insurance
soussigné(e) undersigned
soute *f* hold *(in aircraft)*
spécialiste *m* professional, expert
spécifier specify
sponsoriser sponsor (v)
spot *m* **publicitaire** (TV) commercial
stabiliser stabilize
stabiliser, se level off, level out
stabilité d'emploi security of tenure
stage, jeune cadre en management trainee
stagiaire *m/f* trainee
stagiaire diplômé(e) graduate trainee
standard téléphonique (telephone) switchboard
standardiser standardize
standardiste *m/f* telephonist
statuer rule, give a decision
statut *m* status
statut *m* **légal** legal status
stipulation *f* provision, condition
stipuler stipulate
stock en fin d'exercice closing stock
stock initial/d'ouverture opening stock
stock, en in stock
stocker stock (v) *(goods)*
stratégie *f* strategy, strategic planning
stratégie commerciale marketing strategy
stratégie des affaires business strategy
subvention *f* subsidy
subventionner subsidize
succès, qui a du successful
succès, sans unsuccessful
succession, prendre la take over *(from so.)*

succursale f (d'une banque) branch (of a bank)
suite à further to
suite, prendre la take over (from so.)
suivant depending on
suivant avis as per advice
suivre follow up
suivre une formation train (v) (learn)
superdividende m surplus dividend
superviser supervise
supplément m additional charges, extra charge, surcharge
supprimer delete; cut, reduce
sûr(e) reliable
surabondance f glut, surplus
surbooking m double-booking, overbooking
surbooking, faire un overbook
surcapacité f excess capacity, overcapacity
surface f au sol floor space
surproduction f overproduction
surréservation f double-booking, overbooking
surréserver overbook
surtaxe f (tax) surcharge
surveillance f control, check, supervision
surveillance, de supervisory
surveillant(e) supervisor
surveiller supervise, control
suspendre stop (doing sth.)
syndicaliste m/f trade unionist
syndicat m (trade) union
système informatique computer system

T

tableau m à feuilles mobiles flip chart
tâche f job, task
taille f courante stock size
talent m skill
talon m counterfoil
tarif m rate, tariff; price list
tarif en vigueur going rate
tarif horaire hourly rate
tarif postal postage; postal rate
tarif réduit cheap rate, reduced rate
tarif tout compris all-in price, inclusive charge
tarif unitaire piece rate

tarifs mpl scale of charges
tarifs publicitaires advertising rates
taux m rate, percentage; ratio
taux d'amortissement depreciation rate
taux d'échange en vigueur current rate of exchange
taux d'imposition tax rate
taux de base bancaire bank base rate
taux de change exchange rate, rate of exchange
taux de change à terme forward rate
taux de change défavorable unfavourable/unfavorable exchange rate
taux de croissance growth rate
taux de rendement d'une action dividend yield
taux fixe flat rate
taxe f duty, levy
taxe à l'achat purchase tax
taxe à l'importation import duty
taxe comprise inclusive of tax
taxe payée tax paid
taxe sur la valeur ajoutée (TVA) value added tax (VAT)
taxe sur les ventes sales tax
taxer tax (v)
techniques fpl marchandes merchandizing
télécarte f phone card
télécopie f fax
téléphone à carte card phone
téléphone interne internal telephone
télévision f en circuit fermé closed circuit TV
témoin m witness
témoin, signer en qualité de witness (v) (a document)
temps, à plein full-time
temps complet, à full-time
tendances fpl du marché market forces, market trends
tenir une promesse keep a promise
tenir une réunion/une discussion hold a meeting/a discussion
terme m term (of validity)
terme, à court short-term
terme, à long long-term
terme, à moyen medium-term
termes mpl terms
termes de, aux termes under, according to

terminaison

terminaison *f* expiry, termination
terminal (maritime) pour porte-conteneurs container terminal
terminal d'ordinateur computer terminal
terminer complete (v)
terminer, se end (v)
terrain *m* land
tester test (v)
ticket *m* de caisse receipt, sales slip
tierce personne *f* third party
tiers *m* third party
timbre dateur date stamp
timbre(-poste) *m* (postage) stamp
tiré *m* drawee
tirer un chèque draw a cheque/check
tireur *m* drawer (of cheque/check, etc.)
titre *m* job title
titre au porteur bearer bond
titres *mpl* securities
tonalité *f*(du téléphone) dialling tone
tonalité 'occupé' engaged tone
total général grand total
total reporté running total
touche *f* key (on keyboard)
touche de contrôle control key
touche de majuscules shift key
toucher un chèque cash a cheque/check
tous frais payés all expenses paid
tout de suite immediately
toutes taxes comprises (TTC) inclusive of tax
traducteur (-trice) translator
traduction *f* translation
traduire translate
traite *f* draft (money)
traite à vue sight draft
traite bancaire bank draft
traitement *m* pay, salary
traitement de commandes order processing
traitement de données processing of information
traitement de texte word-processing
traiter handle, deal with, process
traiter une affaire transact business
transaction, effectuer une transact business
transfert *m* transfer
transport *m* transport, carriage
transport par avion air freight

transport, entreprise *f* de carrier (company)
transporter carry, transport
transporteur *m* carrier (company)
transports en commun public transport
transports routiers road transport
travail *m* work; job, employment; piece of work
travail à la pièce/aux pièces piecework
travail à temps partiel/à mi-temps part-time work
travail au noir black economy; moonlighting
travail en cours work in progress
travail en retard/en attente backlog
travail habituel/routinier routine work
travail posté/par équipe shift work
travail rémunérateur well-paid job
travail temporaire casual work
travailler work (v)
travailleur (-euse) worker
treizième mois Christmas bonus
tribunal *m*, tribunaux *mpl* court, law courts
tribunaux, (affaire) devant les sub judice
trimestre *m* quarter (three months)
trimestriel (-elle) quarterly (adj)
troc *m* barter
trois exemplaires, en in triplicate
trop-perçu *m* overcharge, overpayment
troquer barter (v)
trouver des capitaux raise/obtain money
TTC (toutes taxes comprises) inclusive of tax
TVA (taxe sur la valeur ajoutée) VAT (value added tax)

U

unilatéral(e) unilateral
Union européenne (UE) European Union (EU)
unique unique, one-off
urgent(e) urgent
usine *f* factory
usiner manufacture (v)
usure *f* normale wear and tear

utilisateur *m* **(final)** end user
utilisation *f* utilization, use
utiliser use (v)

V

valable valid
valeur *f* value
valeur au pair par value
valeur comptable book value
valeur de l'actif asset value
valeur de reprise trade-in price
valeur déclarée declared value
valeur nette net worth
valeur nominale nominal value, par value, face value
valeurs *fpl* securities
valeurs convertibles convertible loan stock
valide, n'être plus expire, lapse
valoir worth, be worth; cost
varier diversify
vendeur (-euse) shop assistant; vendor; salesman
vendre à terme sell forward
vendre au rabais discount (v)
vendre aux enchères auction (v)
vendre des marchandises au détail retail goods
vendre moins cher qu'un concurrent undercut a rival
vendre, à for sale
vendre à, se retail, sell for *(a price)*
vente *f* sale, disposal, selling
vente au comptant cash sale
vente aux enchères auction
vente directe direct mail/selling
vente forcée forced/distress sale
vente par correspondance (VPC) mail-order
vente réglée par carte de crédit credit card sale
vente, en on sale
ventes *fpl* sales
ventes *fpl* **intérieures** domestic sales, home sales
ventes médiocres low sales
ventes prévues projected sales
ventilation *f* **(des frais)** breakdown (of costs)
ventiler les frais break down/itemize (costs)

vérification *f* verification, control, check
vérification comptable audit (n)
vérifier verify, check, control
vérifier les comptes audit the accounts
versement *m* instalment; payment, amount paid
versement annuel yearly payment
versement forfaitaire lump sum
verser de l'argent pay out
verser de l'argent (sur un compte) deposit money (into an account)
vice *m* **de fabrication** defect
vide empty; vacant
vieux, vieil, vieille old
vigile *m* security guard
vigueur, être en be in operation
virement *m* **bancaire** bank transfer
virement de crédit credit transfer, transfer of funds
virgule *f* **(décimale)** decimal point
visa de transit transit visa
visa permanent (bon pour plusieurs entrées) multiple entry visa
viser (à) aim (to)
visite *f* call, visit
visite impromptue (d'un représentant) cold call
vitrine *f* shop window
voix *f* **prépondérante** casting vote
vol *m* theft; flight *(air)*
vol à l'étalage shoplifting
vol charter charter flight
vol régulier scheduled flight
voleur (-euse) shoplifter
volume *m* capacity *(space)*
volume d'affaires volume of trade, volume of business
vote *m* **par procuration** proxy vote
VPC (vente par correspondance) mail-order
vrac, en loose
VRP (voyageur représentant placier) *m/f* rep (representative)

W, X, Y, Z

warrant *m* warrant
zone franche free trade zone